Also by Anne Willan

Great Cooks and Their Recipes
Grand Diplôme Cooking Course, 20 volume series
French Regional Cooking
La Varenne Pratique
Look & Cook, 17 volume series
Perfect Cookbooks, 9 volume series
Cook It Right
In & Out of the Kitchen in Fifteen Minutes or Less
From My Château Kitchen
Cooking with Wine
Good Food No Fuss
The Good Cook
The Country Cooking of France
The Cookbook Library
One Soufflé at a Time: A Memoir of Food and France
Secrets from the La Varenne Kitchen
How to Cook Absolutely Everything
Best Recipes for Absolutely Everything
Bistro Cooking
French Country Cooking
Château Cuisine
Real Food: Fifty Years of Good Eating
Classic French Cooking
La Varenne's Paris Kitchen
The Observer French Cookery School
La Varenne's Basic French Cookery

WOMEN IN THE KITCHEN

Twelve Essential Cookbook Writers
Who Defined the Way We Eat,
from 1661 to Today

Anne Willan

SCRIBNER

New York   London   Toronto   Sydney   New Delhi

Scribner
An Imprint of Simon & Schuster, Inc.
1230 Avenue of the Americas
New York, NY 10020

First Scribner hardcover edition May 2020

SCRIBNER and design are registered trademarks of The Gale Group, Inc.,
used under license by Simon & Schuster, Inc., the publisher of this work.

For information about special discounts for bulk purchases,
please contact Simon & Schuster Special Sales at 1-866-506-1949
or business@simonandschuster.com.

The Simon & Schuster Speakers Bureau can bring authors to your live event.
For more information or to book an event contact the Simon & Schuster Speakers Bureau
at 1-866-248-3049 or visit our website at www.simonspeakers.com.

Interior design by Erich Hobbing

Manufactured in the United States of America

1   3   5   7   9   10   8   6   4   2

Library of Congress Cataloging-in-Publication Data has been applied for.

ISBN 978-1-5011-7331-8
ISBN 978-1-5011-7333-2 (ebook)

Photo credits: page 153, Irma Rombauer: Bettmann via Getty Images; page 175,
Julia Child: © The Julia Child Foundation for Gastronomy and the Culinary Arts.
Provided courtesy of the Schlesinger Library, Radcliffe Institute, Harvard University; page
211, Edna Lewis: photo by Martha Cooper/New York Post Archives/ © NYP Holdings,
Inc., via Getty Images; page 237, Marcella Hazan: courtesy of Victor Hazan; page 259,
Alice Waters: courtesy of MasterClass.

To Mark who collected these books.

From Anne who uses them.

Very much love

CONTENTS

ACKNOWLEDGMENTS

I wish to thank:

Lisa Ekus, my agent who so happily joined me with Kara Watson, my wonderfully helpful editor at Scribner. Thanks also to Kate Slate for her careful copyedits and the rest of the team at Scribner.

Todd Schulkin, editor, manager, and friend, who has guided this book through proposal to contract, to final manuscript and printed text.

Susan Broussard, whose watchful eye in the La Varenne kitchen ensured that my modern versions of recipes from twelve historical cooks work perfectly with today's ingredients. She had the enthusiastic help of staff members Nicole Litvak, Daylin Ramirez, and Elizabeth Weinstein.

Lauren Salkeld's sharp eye and insight in editing the final recipe text has been invaluable.

Alexandra Wright has edited the final text, uniting text and recipes to complete the finished manuscript with great dexterity and skill. She has also dealt so patiently with my last-minute inspirations.

Working with all of you has been such a pleasure.

WOMEN IN
THE KITCHEN

A woman cook bastes meat on a spit in front of the open fire.
On the table behind her lies a cookbook with instructions
for the task at hand. In the background, a male server
takes plates out to the unseen dinner table.

INTRODUCTION

Over the centuries, millions of women have cooked in the kitchen but far fewer have written down what they learned. And far, far fewer have seen their words in print. The first woman's cookbook published in English was *The Queen-like Closet, or Rich Cabinet* by Hannah Woolley. It appeared in 1670, less than six years after a great fire destroyed most of medieval London. The urge to document what still existed must have been compelling, and in a supplement to the 1681 edition Mrs. Woolley observes:

> Ladies, I hope your pleas'd and so shall I,
> If what I've Writ, you may be gainers by:
> If not; it is your fault, it is not mine,
> Your benefit in this I do design.
> Much labour and much time it hath me cost;
> Therefore I beg, let none of it be lost.

The underlying motive for writing a cookbook has not varied over the years: it is to document recipes, including both ingredients and cooking methods, for current reference and to be handed down to future generations. In *A New System of Domestic Cookery* for example, published in 1806, Maria Rundell recorded the principles of household management for her three daughters, a book that circulated widely throughout the 1800s on both sides of the Atlantic. She wanted to pass down her own knowledge, and a similar urge to share the joys of cooking, of getting the texture, appearance, and flavor just right, has inspired so many cooks to write down what they have learned.

This book about women in the kitchen is informed by a collection

3

of two-thousand-plus cookbooks that, thanks to my husband, Mark Cherniavsky, was built up over the more than fifty years I have been writing about cooking. Many of the books are by men, but most of the active, recipe books, the ones I take into the kitchen, are by women. They begin with Hannah Woolley, who was a sort of auntie offering hints on makeup and medicine, crochet and cookery. Her six children I'm sure thrived on her Scotch Collops, Bisket Cakes, Candied Carrots, Gooseberry Fool, Pippin Pies, and other such delights.

Ever since working at *Gourmet* magazine in the early 1960s, I have developed the habit of assessing an author's recipes: Are they clear and precise, can you see the food on the plate, and, above all, would you want to eat it? Myself, I cannot resist the brilliant, erratic Hannah Glasse who eloped at age sixteen with a junior army officer and was briefly dressmaker to the king's sister, Princess Charlotte, and whose *The Art of Cookery Made Plain and Easy* (1747) dominated the field of English cookbooks for more than fifty years. Then there is Amelia Simmons whose *American Cookery* (1796) sums up the hardscrabble kitchen of early New England with such clarity. And in the last fifty years come the cooks I knew personally, authoritative Marcella Hazan, Julia Child who was a close friend (and a second grandmother to my own children), and now Alice Waters who shares my affinity for France.

I have chosen twelve cookbook authors and each is described in a biography followed by a handful of their own recipes as they appeared in the original, together with those same recipes adapted for the modern kitchen. Together these books trace the development of domestic cookery in England and America as recorded by women, whose position and career paths in both countries were very different from that of men. The general cooking style of women was different, too: Women's recipes tend to be simpler, warm-hearted, easier to execute, requiring less equipment, and calling for less expensive ingredients. Women cooks mark festivities, with recipes like A Rich Plumb Cake, or Election Pie—a cold savory meat pie best prepared well in advance so the flavor mellows. It is often the women in the kitchen who set the scene, and establish the family tastes, particularly of the children. I think of my mother's crispy ginger biscuits that, more than seventy years ago, I learned to dip in a mug of hot milky tea.

INTRODUCTION

The ability to write a cookbook presupposes a certain education, which was by no means common for girls before the nineteenth century. A woman cookbook author was likely to come from a small family with a sufficient income for extras, including the spare time to sit down and record recipes. Nine of the women in this book were married and six had children. Domestic cooking was done predominantly by women, whereas men were most often found in professional and commercial kitchens. Men's cooking tended to be more complicated, affected by trends, and designed to please strangers as often as family and friends. It was no accident that during the eighteenth century the term *chef* meaning "leader" was applied to the male head cook of a large kitchen. The title was not used for women until the 1960s and the television shows of Julia Child, when the lines on who was cooking in which sphere started to blur.

Hannah Woolley takes the lead as the first English woman to have her book printed. Her cookbook (she wrote several more general books) would certainly have been based on a handwritten notebook, perhaps passed down in the family, that Hannah relied on in the kitchen and about the house, hence the remedies for Cough of the Lungs and Pain in the Bones that are scattered here and there among the Puddings and Candies. It is little surprise that most cookbooks were written when their authors were in their forties, often older—it takes time to accumulate a stock of delicious, time-tested recipes. Most early authors were from the middle class, prosperous enough to experiment in the kitchen, but not wealthy. As authors, in publishing their recipes in a cookbook, not only did they distribute their ideas to a wider audience, the book was a promotional tool for businesses such as the Fannie Farmers cooking school. An exception is the Southern American plantation owner Sarah Rutledge, who penned her personal cookbook to instruct her cooks, and had it printed as an indulgence for the pleasure of her friends and to aid in the running of their own households.

Many cookbook writers were idealistic in their wish to pass on their knowledge, and in later centuries women like Fannie Farmer, Julia Child, and Marcella Hazan opened cooking schools and gave classes. Each of them defined a regional cuisine in her cookbook—American, French, and Italian—and they all shared the same insistence on technique. In 1975, I myself followed in their shoes, opening a cooking school in Paris called La Varenne in honor of François Pierre de la Varenne, cook and author of the first French cookbook, published in 1651 and outlining what is still considered classic French cuisine. Julia and her husband, Paul Child, had a hand in helping us settle on La Varenne as the school's name.

The motive of other authors in writing cookbooks was more practical. Hannah Glasse, a champion saleswoman and briefly dressmaker to the Princess of Wales, was feckless with money and for months she was jailed for debt. She hit upon the idea of publishing her own recipes for the fashionable world she encountered in London. The book was sold in a chic china shop and its success was such that *The Art of Cookery Made Plain and Easy* (1747) remained without rival until the end of the century. In America, the nineteenth-century writer Lydia Child, an intellectual who wrote dozens of books on all sorts of subjects to keep her family finances afloat, also wrote her cookbook for the money.

Once a book is published, it must earn an audience. The readership of early books would have been modest, after all far fewer people, especially women, could read. But Hannah Woolley was sufficiently renowned for a publisher to have launched four of her books. Maria Rundell was lucky enough to know the family of John Murray, a publishing house that still exists. In America, Amelia Simmons had such success with *American Cookery* that it was printed in eight different New England towns, starting in Hartford in 1796 and ending in New York in 1822. Later in the century, the aristocratic Sarah Rutledge had a built-in audience of friends and visitors at the ready when she published *The Carolina Housewife*, her household notebook of recipes, in Charleston, South Carolina. Moving to the present day, *Joy of Cooking* by Irma Rombauer has sold more than seven million copies and counting as it is still in print. Today's media have revolutionized cookbook sales, for example the movie *Julie & Julia* so boosted the sales of *Mastering the Art of French Cooking* that, on August 23, 2009, the book briefly appeared on the *New York Times* bestseller list for nonfiction, a first for any cookbook.

The voice of a gifted cookery writer sounds as strong in a recipe as in prose. "Before you set your Milk," remarks Mrs. Woolley, when making junket (the nursery dessert), "You may if you please, colour it with the juice of Marigolds, Spinage, or Sage." Just imagine having a little pot of each color on your plate! A talented author does not just give instructions, she adds her vision of the finished dish with, in later centuries, observations about the seasons and appropriate occasions: "All roads lead to the home, *la cucina casereccia*," declares Marcella Hazan of the cooking of Italy, while Edna Lewis adds a reminiscence or two of harvest time in the 1930s in the fields of Virginia: "When dinner was ready," remarks Edna, "one of the cooks would go out and ring a giant dinner bell so that it could be heard all over the countryside. And the men would gather hungrily around the tables that were laden with so many good things: boiled pork shoulder, braised beef, fried chicken with gravy, baked tenderloin, new cabbage, pork-flavored beans, hot spiced beets, baked tomatoes, potato salad, corn pudding, an assortment of pickles, hot corn batter bread, biscuits. . . ." It is the voice of an outstanding cookbook writer as much as her recipes that mark her brilliance and ability to withstand the test of time.

Note: The modern recipes in this book were tested with US ingredients including all-purpose unbleached wheat flour, granulated (UK castor) sugar, unsalted butter, and Grade A large eggs.

In *Women in the Kitchen* you will find women from all walks of life, from a self-declared orphan to an aristocrat daughter of a signer of the Declaration of Independence to modern women who have blazed professional trails of their own. They were (and are) all strong-minded and many of them had to finance the publication and printing costs of the books they had written, especially in the early days. All had to have the initiative and find the time to write down their recipes, assemble them in coherent order, and then arrange for distribution. These were leaders of their time, determined to instruct their fellow cooks and, more important, to instill the love as well as the learning of good cooking. They have influenced, inspired, altered, and perfected what has come to be contemporary food writing, the modern cookbook, and the way we eat today. Long may they continue to do so!

HANNAH WOOLLEY

1622–1675

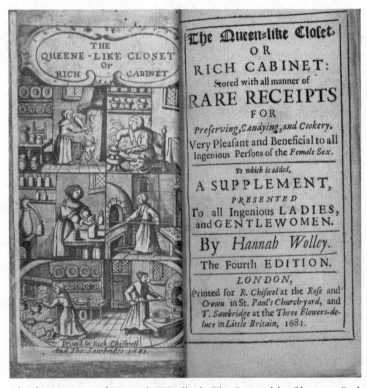

The frontispiece of Hannah Woolley's *The Queen-like Closet, or Rich Cabinet* shows the cook from top left filling a cauldron, beating sauce over a brazier, working in the stillroom, setting bread in the oven, and a general view of two women at work in the kitchen.

RECIPES

Chapter 1

HANNAH WOOLLEY

The Queen-like Closet, or Rich Cabinet

*This first cookbook by a woman, in English, leads the way
for future cooks in the domestic kitchen.*

The first handbook written in English by a woman for women was published in 1661, almost two hundred years after the first cookbook was printed (in Latin). In *The Ladies Directory*, Hannah Woolley began to reveal not just her own life but a whole new world for her readers, that of the expanding English middle class of prosperous tradesmen, physicians, and the like, all of them profiting from the newly restored monarchy of King Charles II. In a group of later books Woolley elaborated on the skills called for in the domestic kitchen, a very different world from the grand establishments of the professional male cooks who had hitherto dominated the cookbook scene.

Hannah's audience was the mistress of the house who did the work in the kitchen, often with her daughters, backed up perhaps by a scullery maid. Before *The Ladies Directory*, no printed cookbook had existed for the English housewife. If she were lucky, she could turn to a "commonplace" book of handwritten recipes and notes passed down to her from a previous generation, to which she would add her own comments and ideas. But a printed book of domestic instruction with actual recipes for cooking was very new.

Hannah Woolley went on to write four more books over ten years, all of them household manuals, with digressions into beauty tips and even the art of fishing. The feminine focus is reflected in their titles: *The Cooks Guide* (1664); *The Queen-like Closet, or Rich Cabinet* (1670); and *The Gentlewoman's Companion or, a Guide to the Female Sex* (1673). In all her titles, she mentions "Ladies," "Gentlewomen," or even "Female Sex," declaring in the preface of her last book "I hope it may deserve the Title of *The Accomplish'd Ladies Delight* [1675] and may acquire Acceptance at your Fair Hands, whereby you will very much Encourage and Oblige." She has the invaluable gift of appealing directly to her market, a very modern approach.

Hannah must have been a voracious taker of notes, with one of those inquiring minds that strays from subject to subject with delightful inconsequence. Certainly she would have kept a commonplace book of remedies, cooking and household hints, with special treats such as raspberry wine and white sugar candies. She focuses on cookery, though *The Ladies Directory* jumps about with recipes for "Consumption" and the "Chin-cough" among the cakes and cordials. Her books were filled with her own knowledge—useful, somewhat disorganized information on cooking, running a house, and keeping the family healthy and well fed. "A cordial to cause sleep" might follow "To perfume gloves" and "To preserve cherries in jelly."

Like many women of her time, Hannah was skilled in "Physick" to which she added "Chirurgery" (work as a physician). Her mother and elder sisters were also involved in medicine, though nothing is known of her father. From 1639 to 1646, Hannah was employed as a servant, more likely a kind of apprentice in a great house—probably that of Lady Anne Maynard, who lived near Hannah's family home of Newport in Essex, a village forty miles north of London. Lady Maynard remained a friend to Hannah and perhaps subsidized the free grammar school run by Jerome Woolley (sometimes spelled Wolley), whom Hannah married in 1646. The couple had at least four sons and two daughters; a comparatively small family for the time, and the marriage was depicted by Hannah as a happy one.

Jerome died in 1661 and five years later Hannah was married again to Francis Challiner at St. Margaret's, Westminster, a fashionable address. In 1670, her most successful cookbook, *The Queen-like Closet, or Rich Cabinet: Stored with all manner of Rare Receipts*, was published. ("Closets," "cabinets," and "secrets" were buzzwords of the time.) It ran several editions, including translations into German, and concentrated on the kitchen—unlike her earlier books that digressed into medicine and beauty care. Mrs. Woolley had earned a reputation as a successful physician, despite her amateur status and the unwelcoming environment for female medical practitioners at that time. She used her books as an advertisement for her skills, and invited her readers to consult her in person.

The kitchen in which Mrs. Woolley worked is vividly illustrated in the frontispiece vignettes of her *Queen-like Closet*. Here again is the emphasis on cooking for women housewives, so different from that of male professional cooks. The hem of her skirt leaves her slippered feet free, and her arms are protected by long sleeves. Her hair is shielded from steam and sparks in a bonnet (each one makes a different fashion statement) and a long apron is tied around her waist to keep clean what was probably her only dress. She is at work filling a cauldron, beating a sauce over a brazier, working in the stillroom, and setting bread in the oven with the long-handled shovel called a peel (from the French *pelle*). Thank heaven for today's electric food processors, choppers, and slicers that help with these back-breaking tasks. How lucky we are!

By 1670 Hannah was a well-known author and probably lived in London. She had gained an influential patroness, a Mrs. Grace Buzby, "Daughter to Sir HENRY CARY, Knight Banneret," to whom *Queen-like Closet* is dedicated. Wanting to appeal to a wide audience, Hannah announced that her "Bills of Fare" were for "Great Houses," in one of which she had trained, and also for "Houses of Lesser Quality," just as she lived at home. Still, times must sometimes have been hard, as she laments in the book:

> *I sit here sad while you{r} are merry,*
> *Eating Dainties, drinking Perry;*
> *But I'm content you should so feed,*
> *So I may have to serve my need.*

By today's standards, Hannah Woolley's books may seem confusing, but she includes all the elements we think essential to a modern cookbook—a trendy title, an alluring frontispiece, an author's statement of purpose, and an index. The recipes may lack many of the attributes we think important such as ingredient quantities, but her instructions would have been intelligible to an experienced cook. As for serving amounts, in Hannah's day a variety of dishes were laid out on the table for all to help themselves or be served by passing plates from hand to hand. For more diners, more dishes would be added, so that the number of people to be served by a given recipe, as is the norm in today's cookbooks, was scarcely relevant.

Mrs. Woolley's focus was on the practical instructions: "Take your artichokes before they are overgrown, or too full of strings, and when they are pared round, that nothing is left but the bottom, boyl them till they be indifferent tender, but not full boyled . . . ," she says. And of an Eel-Pye: "if you please, you may put in some Raisins of the Sun, and some large Mace, it is good hot or cold." She had an eye for novelty and the very first mention in a cookbook of "chaculato," the magic ingredient from the New World that was to sweep the dessert table in following centuries, comes in *The Queen-like Closet*, recipe 162, where she simmers a chocolate drink with claret wine, thickening it with egg yolks and sweetening it with sugar. (Chocolate arrived in Europe first as a drink, and it was decades before it was used to flavor other dishes.)

Hannah borrows from at least one earlier author, Sir Hugh Plat, who like other gentlemen enjoyed experimenting in his "elaboratory," a sort of kitchen. At the time, plagiarism was not regarded so unkindly as now, though copyright was recognized and enforced. Imitation was thought of as a way of passing on to others the best of the best. Hannah was not averse to plagiarizing herself, occasionally repeating recipes from book to book, perhaps because they filled a gap or she particularly liked them.

In 1675, almost at the end of Hannah Woolley's life, *The Accomplish'd Ladies Delight* was published, devoted to "Preserving, Physick, Beautifying, and Cookery." The frontispiece includes another handsome portrait, perhaps of the author, her hair dressed with curling irons in the latest style. On the title page are illustrations of a stillroom, a lady at her dressing table, and a working kitchen, together summing up the breadth of Hannah Woolley's expertise. Her name brought money and an unauthorized title, *The Accomplish'd Lady's Delight in Preserving, Physick, Beautifying, and Cookery* (1675) appeared falsely under her name. *The Compleat Servant-maid: Or, the Young Maiden's and Family's daily Companion*, appeared in 1729, so long after Mrs. Woolley's death as surely to be merely trading on her reputation. Her name as author made the book a bestseller, though most if not all of *The Accomplish'd Ladies* text is believed to be written by others. As a sure sign of success, her books started to be plagiarized by other authors in such titles as *The Compleat Servant-Maid* (1677). Most of her books must have crossed the Atlantic to colonial America.

Woolley's work stands out, reflected in her book sales in a market dominated by men. She firmly established a woman's authorial competence. Nonetheless, her success was slow to inspire others and only one new cookbook by a woman appeared in England before the turn of the seventeenth century. However, this was a winner: *Rare and Excellent Receipts, Experienced and Taught* by Mrs. Mary Tillinghast was published in London in 1678. As the title implies, Mrs. Tillinghast ran cookery schools, a genre that flourishes today, leading to countless book-of-the-school cookbooks.

After 1700, more cookbooks by women writers gradually began to appear, but just four in the first half of the century, a slow start for what was to become a surging tide of cookbooks written in English by women. Mrs. Woolley was a pioneer, it was her somewhat erratic example that led the way to the plethora of domestic printed cookbooks to come. She enabled me, three centuries later, to write an illustrated series of cookbooks that were translated into eighteen different languages and sold millions of copies, and I am by no means the only cook who has done so. The shape our books have taken, and their ultimate success, can be directly traced back to Hannah Woolley, proof of her abundant talent and leadership. She was onto a good thing.

THE HEAT OF THE MATTER:
THE HEARTH

Early recipes such as Hannah Woolley's were cooked over an open fire, which from the fifteenth century onward was increasingly often set on a stone or heatproof brick hearth and vented by a chimney. This fireplace had to be tall enough for the cook to stand more or less upright under the mantel beam, with the hearth proportionately wide. At the back, a cast-iron chimney plate would reflect and intensify the heat of the fire.

The basic utensil in an open hearth was a large cauldron with its pothook dangling from a chain on a rotating metal arm within the chimney. The pothook was equipped with a ratchet to adjust the cauldron height over the embers. The cook also had a roasting spit, a simple rod with a drip pan, perched on two supports and a handle, calling for muscle power to keep it turning. Like any open fire today, the traditional hearth had its accessories of tongs, ladles, forks, spoons, brushes, and shovels for the ashes, with cloths for handling the hot pots. Well-dried logs, large and small, were stacked beside the fireplace, some quick burning, others of dense hardwood whose embers would last through the night. For light, a small niche in the back wall of the chimney might have housed a candlestick.

Judging from the frontispiece of *The Queen-like Closet*, Mrs. Woolley's kitchen was one of the elite that included a built-in oven, a smaller version of today's pizza ovens. The oven has a characteristic domed shape, with an arched opening and the floor at waist height. To heat the inside, embers and kindling sticks from the main fire are spread on the oven floor, warming the interior. The high temperature needed for certain items such as bread rolls or butter pastries can take several hours to achieve. Once hot, the embers are raked to one side and the oven cools gradually. In an active kitchen it will never be allowed to get cold, but used for toasting bread crumbs or drying herbs. Reheating is thus all the quicker.

To pickle Oysters

The Queen-like Closet, or Rich Cabinet, 1681

Take your great Oysters, and in opening them, save the liquor, then strain it from dross, add it to some White Wine, and White Wine Vinegar, and a little Salt, and so let them boil together awhile, putting in whole Mace, whole Cloves, whole Pepper, Sliced Ginger, and quartered Nutmegs; with a few Bay Leaves; when the Liquor is boiled almost enough, put in your Oysters and plump them, then lay them out to cool, then put them into a Gally-pot or Barrel, and when the Liquor is cool, pour it over them, and keep them from the air.

PICKLED OYSTERS

Hannah Woolley makes generous use of oysters, pickling them as well as simmering them as oyster stew, adding them to "sea pie," using them almost as a condiment in meat pies, even pairing them with chicken and the gravy for roast lamb. Clearly they were very, very plentiful and cheap.

Any oysters, briny or mild, plump or small, can be pickled and they keep well in the refrigerator for at least a week. I like to warm them for a minute or two, then drain and serve them on buttered whole wheat toast as a snack or first course for dinner. They are an excellent addition to fish stews or a side garnish for a Bloody Mary.

SERVES 4

2 cups/500 ml dry white wine
2 cups/500 ml white wine vinegar or cider vinegar
1-inch/2.5 cm piece fresh ginger, peeled and sliced
3 to 4 blades mace

2 to 3 bay leaves
1 tablespoon black peppercorns
1 teaspoon whole cloves
1 teaspoon salt
1 quart/1 liter freshly shucked oysters, with their liquor
1 whole nutmeg
1 lemon, halved and very thinly sliced
2-quart/2-liter jar

1. In a large, shallow saucepan, combine the wine, vinegar, ginger, mace, bay leaves, peppercorns, cloves, and salt. Drain the oysters and add the liquor to the pan. Stir the pickling juice, bring to a boil to make a stock, and simmer until reduced by about half, 4 to 5 minutes.

2. Meanwhile, put the nutmeg in a plastic bag, crush it with a rolling pin, and add to the stock.

3. Add the oysters to the stock and bring back to just a simmer. If the oysters are large, simmer 30 more seconds; if small, stop cooking. Immediately drain the oysters in a colander set over a bowl to catch the stock. Discard the spices.

4. Layer the oysters in the jar with the sliced lemon and pour in the reserved stock. Seal the jar and refrigerate at least 24 hours so the oysters mellow. The pickled oysters will keep 1 to 2 weeks in the refrigerator.

To make boiled Sallads

The Queen-like Closet, or Rich Cabinet, 1681

Boil some Carrots very tender & scrape them to pieces like The Pulp of an Apple; and Season them with Cinnamon, Ginger and Sugar, put in Currants, a little Vinegar, and a piece of Sweet Butter, stew these in a dish, and when they begin to dry, put in more Butter and a little Salt, so serve them to the Table; thus you may do Lettuce or Spinage or Beets.

SPICED CARROT PURÉE

To our palates, this "sallad" tastes more like carrot cake than a salad. Thoroughly boiled carrots are mashed to a purée, then cooked again with sugar, spice, salt, and a sweet-sour touch of vinegar and dried currants (currants were a favorite flavoring of the time). Carrot purée is perfect with winter stews or the Thanksgiving turkey.

SERVES 4

6 medium carrots (about 1 pound/450 g), trimmed and peeled
1 tablespoon butter, diced, more to finish
1 tablespoon white wine vinegar or cider vinegar, or to taste
1 tablespoon sugar, or to taste
1 tablespoon dried currants
1 teaspoon ground cinnamon
1 teaspoon ground ginger
Pinch of salt, or to taste

1. Cut the carrots into ½-inch/1 cm chunks. Put them in a saucepan with water to cover generously and bring to a boil. Simmer until tender, 20 to 30 minutes, depending on the age of the carrots. Drain

in a colander. When cool, crush the carrots in the saucepan with a potato masher until quite finely puréed. Stir in the butter, vinegar, sugar, currants, cinnamon, ginger, and salt.

2. Place the saucepan over medium heat and cook, stirring constantly, until the purée is hot and fragrant, 4 to 5 minutes. Remove from the heat and stir in more diced butter if you wish. Taste the purée and adjust the seasoning with spice, sugar, vinegar, and salt. Serve hot or warm.

To make a Pompion Pie

The Queen-like Closet, or Rich Cabinet, 1681

Having your Paste ready in your Pan, put in your Pompion pared and cut in thin slices, then fill up your Pie with sharp Apples, and a little Pepper, and a little Salt, then close it and bake it, then butter it, and serve it in hot to the Table.

SAVORY PUMPKIN AND APPLE PIE

In this double-crust pie, sliced pumpkin is topped with tart apples and seasoned only with salt and pepper, and no trace of sugar. The resulting pie is lively, and makes an excellent accompaniment to roast turkey or chicken breast. Hannah calls for "a little Pepper," but I prefer a more generous amount and use freshly ground black pepper. For me, this recipe invites a classic English pie dough made with butter and lard, but don't hesitate to use your own favorite pastry. It's fine to pick up ready-sliced fresh pumpkin pieces at the market—you'll avoid a tough job!

SERVES 6 to 8

For the dough
3 cups/375 g flour, more for rolling
1 teaspoon salt
½ cup/110 g butter, more for the pan
½ cup/110 g lard
6 to 8 tablespoons/90 to 125 ml cold water

For the filling
1 small pumpkin (about 2½ pounds/1.13 kg)
3 tart medium apples (about 2½ pounds/1.13 kg)
½ teaspoon salt, or to taste

1½ teaspoons freshly ground black pepper, or to taste
1 to 2 tablespoons butter, melted, to finish
9-inch/23 cm pie pan

1. Make the dough: In a bowl, stir the flour with the salt. Add the butter and lard and cut them into small pieces using two table knives, one in each hand. Rub the fat into the flour with your fingertips until the mixture resembles crumbs. Sprinkle with 4 tablespoons/60 ml cold water and continue mixing until the dough starts to stick together, adding more water if the crumbs seem dry. Press the dough together in a ball, wrap in a kitchen towel, and refrigerate 10 to 15 minutes.

2. Prepare the filling: With a large chef's knife, cut the skin off the top and bottom of the pumpkin. Angle the knife and work from top to bottom to cut off the remaining skin in strips. Halve the pumpkin, discard the seeds, and cut the flesh into ⅛-inch/3 mm slices.

3. Peel, quarter, and core the apples, then slice them slightly thicker than the pumpkin. There should be about the same volume each of pumpkin and apple slices.

4. To shape the pie, butter the pie pan. Sprinkle a work surface generously with flour. Divide the dough in half. Roll one half to a 9-inch/23 cm round, then line the pan and prick the dough all over with a fork.

5. Arrange the pumpkin slices in the pan, overlapping them like the petals of a flower. Sprinkle with half of the salt and black pepper. Cover the pumpkin with overlapping slices of apple, starting at the edge of the pie and arranging the slices overlapping from the edge. This arrangement helps hold the pie together. Sprinkle the apple slices with the remaining salt and pepper. Brush the rim of the pie dough with water. Roll out the remaining dough to an 11-inch/28 cm round, cover the pie, and seal the edges together with your fingers. Trim off the excess dough and use it to make decorative leaves for the top of the pie. Cut small vent holes with

scissors for steam to escape. Refrigerate the pie until the dough is firm, 15 to 20 minutes.

6. Heat the oven to 400°F/200°C and set a rack low down.

7. Bake the pie for 15 minutes, then reduce the temperature to 350°F/175°C and continue baking until the pie is browned and the filling is very tender in the center when pierced with a skewer, 45 to 55 minutes longer. Serve the pie hot or at room temperature, brushing it with melted butter just before serving.

To make fine Jumbals

Accomplish'd Ladies Delight, 1683

Beat a pound of Sugar fine, then take the same quantity of fine Wheat Flower, and mix them together, then take two whites and one Yolk of an Egg, half a quarter of a pound of Blanched Almonds, then beat them very fine altogether, with half a pound of sweet Butter, and a spoonful of Rose-water, and so work it with a little Cream till it come to a stiff Paste, then roul them forth as you please; you may add a few fine dryed Aniseeds finely rub'd, and strewed into the paste, with Coriander-seeds.

JUMBLED SPICE COOKIES

"Jumbles," sometimes referring to cookies, sometimes cakes, are popular items in old cookbooks, making use of whatever ingredients happen to be around in a working kitchen. For shiny cookies, brush the tops before baking with a syrup made from 2 tablespoons sugar heated in 2 tablespoons water.

MAKES ABOUT THREE DOZEN COOKIES

4 cups/500 g flour, more for rolling

2¼ cups/450 g sugar

1 egg

1 egg white

¼ cup/30 g ground almonds

2 sticks/1 cup/225 g butter, diced, more for the baking sheet

1 to 2 tablespoons heavy cream, more if needed

1 tablespoon rose water

2 teaspoons aniseeds

2 teaspoons coriander seeds

3½-inch/9 cm round cookie cutter

1. In a stand mixer fitted with the paddle, mix the flour and sugar together. Beat in the whole egg, egg white, and ground almonds until mixed to dry crumbs. Add the butter, heavy cream, rose water, aniseeds, and coriander seeds and beat to form crumbs that stick together as a dough. If the crumbs seem dry, add a tablespoon or two more cream.

2. Heat the oven to 350°F/175°C and set a shelf in the center. Line a baking sheet with parchment paper.

3. Sprinkle a work surface lightly with flour and roll the cookie dough to an ⅛-inch/3 mm thickness. Cut out 3½-inch/9 cm rounds with the cookie cutter and set them on the baking sheet. If you like, brush the rounds with sugar syrup. Bake until lightly browned, 12 to 15 minutes.

4. Transfer the cookies to a rack to cool—they will crisp as they cool. Jumbles will keep several days in an airtight container at room temperature. Wrap them tightly as cookies dry out in the open air.

To make good Almond Milk

The Queen-like Closet, or Rich Cabinet, 1681

Take Jordan Almonds blanched and beaten with Rosewater, then strain them often with fair water, wherein hath been boiled Violet Leaves and sliced Dates; when your Almonds are strained, take the Dates and put to it some Mace, Sugar, and a little Salt, warm it a little, and so to drink it.

ALMOND MILK WITH VIOLET LEAVES AND DATES

Now a popular dairy alternative, in Hannah Woolley's time almond milk would have been regarded as a healthy posset, a remedy for the sick. Jordan almonds are our familiar blanched almonds, easy to find still whole and with maximum flavor. Violet leaves come from the same plant whose flowers are so fragrant. The dried leaves are available online and make excellent tea, as well as perfuming this almond "milk." The leaves of sweet geranium would be a good substitute, with nutmeg used instead of the ground mace. Dates were a favorite sweetener of the time.

MAKES 3 CUPS/750 ML ALMOND MILK

2 to 3 tablespoons/about 15 g dried violet leaves

1 quart/1 liter water

8 to 12 dried dates, about 5 ounces/150 g, pitted and sliced

1 cup/170 g whole blanched almonds

2 to 3 teaspoons rose water

½ teaspoon ground mace

Small pinch of salt

1 to 2 teaspoons sugar (optional)

Cheesecloth

1. Tie the violet leaves in a doubled bag of cheesecloth, then combine with the water and dates in a saucepan and simmer until fragrant, 10 to 15 minutes. Let cool to tepid, then discard the violet leaves and strain out the dates, reserving them and the water.

2. With a large knife, coarsely chop the almonds. Put them in a blender, along with the rose water and 1 cup/250 ml of the reserved violet and date water. Pulse to make a moist paste. Add the dates and half of the remaining water and work until smooth, 2 to 3 seconds. Stir the almond and date mixture into the remaining reserved water.

3. Line a sieve with a double layer of cheesecloth and set over a bowl. Work the almond milk through the sieve, squeezing the cheesecloth to extract maximum flavor. Stir in the mace and salt and warm the milk until hot to your fingertip. Taste and sweeten with sugar if needed. Serve warm or at room temperature.

HANNAH GLASSE

1708–1770

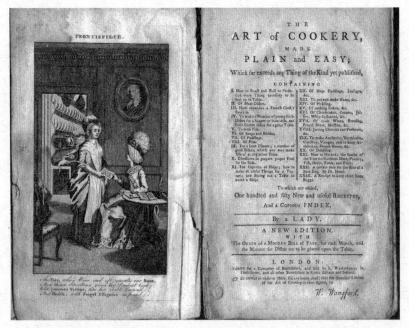

The frontispiece from *The Art of Cookery Made Plain and Easy* shows the lady of the household handing the cook a menu.

RECIPES

A Green Peas-Soop, page 40

To make Force-Meat Balls, page 42

To Pot Salmon, page 44

To Stew a Turky, or Fowl, in Sellery-Sauce, page 46

To make Chocolate Cream, page 49

To make Syrup of Roses, page 51

Big and Baby Green Pea Soup, page 40

Veal Meatballs, page 42

Potted Salmon, page 44

Whole Turkey in Celery Sauce, page 46

Chocolate Pudding with Rosemary, page 49

Rose Petal Syrup, page 51

Chapter 2

HANNAH GLASSE

The Art of Cookery Made Plain and Easy

*The great cookbook of the eighteenth century
that portrays the table of the prosperous English household
for the adventurous cook.*

The Art of Cookery Made Plain and Easy by Hannah Glasse, first published in 1747, was the most influential cookbook of the 1700s, printed in more than twenty editions by the end of the century. This success story is a far cry from the scattershot approach of her predecessor Hannah Woolley but nonetheless owes a good deal to Mrs. Woolley's acute perception of the domestic kitchens of the English middle class. Hannah Glasse was not diverted by cosmetics and perfumes, and rarely with remedies, but focused on cookery. She reveled in the cakes and pastries, the pickles and preserves, the "little made dishes" that enliven a stalwart English foundation of roast meats and fish (no English town is farther than sixty-five miles from the sea), with poultry and some basic vegetables raised in the backyard.

Hannah Glasse's background story reads like one of the romantic novels so popular in her time. She was born in 1708, the illegitimate daughter of an English country gentleman, Isaac Allgood, her mother said to have been a local widow named Hannah Reynolds. These were lenient times and young Hannah was brought up beside her legitimate brothers, Lancelot and another Isaac. Sir Isaac was wealthy but the

Allgood estate in Northumberland was windblown and remote; Hannah was sent to live with her grandmother in London and from there, in 1724 at the age of sixteen, she eloped and married a lieutenant on half-pay, a feckless though presumably charming character called John Glasse.

Lieutenant Glasse was Irish, in the service of the Earl of Donegal at Broomfield in Essex, where the young couple settled, he on half-pay, she with a small annuity of £30 from her half-brother. Here, and later in London, their eleven children were born, though six died in infancy. Hannah Glasse was full of initiative. In a letter of November 1744, she mentions the idea (not pursued) of marketing a patent medicine called Dr. Lower's tincture, that went on to great success as Daffy's elixir. In 1747, when *The Art of Cookery* was published, Mrs. Glasse arranged for the book to be sold at Mrs. Ashburn's china shop at the corner of Fleet-Ditch in London. That same year Mrs. Glasse set up as a dressmaker with her daughter Margaret (trained as a milliner) and attracted some distinguished visitors.

In the first three editions, the author of *The Art of Cookery* was listed simply as "By a Lady"—a not uncommon subterfuge but titillating all the same. The book was sufficiently notable as to draw the attention of Dr. Samuel Johnson, man of letters and author of the pioneer English dictionary, who is quoted as saying drily "women can spin very well, but they cannot make a good book of cookery." In the fourth edition a clue appeared with the signature H. Glasse scribbled next to By a Lady but no one knew who Mrs. Glasse was. Then, in the 1751 edition of *The Art of Cookery*, a full-page notice advertised a certain Hannah Glasse as "Dressmaker to the Princess of Wales." The secret was out, and that was how the matter rested for more than two centuries. In 1938 historian Madeline Hope Dodds noticed that the imposing list of more than two hundred subscribers to the first edition of *The Art of Cookery* was headed by a certain Mrs. ALLGOOD, the name in capitals. The unusual name quickly led to Northumberland and the discovery of Hannah's origins. Subscribers guaranteed payment to the printer, thus subsidizing the first copies of the book.

Whoever financed the first edition of *The Art of Cookery* spared no expense, and the resulting octavo volume, with its heavy paper and generous margins, is a pleasure to behold. This edition was the foundation of the library of cookbooks that my husband and I began collecting when we were married in 1966. Even then, a couple of decades before collecting cookbooks became a popular hobby, it was a serious investment for a young married couple. But it was worth it. We were entranced by the mixture of italic and roman type larded with capitals on every noun, with the long "s" so easily confused with an "f" that seems clumsy by our standards but is not hard to follow. At Mrs. Glasse's suggestion I still use rosemary to flavor chocolate pudding, and a straggly little rosemary bush does surprisingly well on my balcony in north London. Mrs. Glasse does not provide an alphabetical index but she lists the recipes by page and in order of chapter, calling for a sharp eye to search the nearly one thousand recipes dotted among twenty-two chapters. Later editions added a more conventional index.

Hannah Glasse's success with her book was short-lived; she was a fine publicist but not a sound businesswoman. John Glasse once lamented "she does not calculate well as I could wish in many things." Soon she was cashing in her only reliable source of income, the family annuity. In May 1754 Hannah was declared bankrupt to the amount of £10,000, a considerable fortune at the time. In 1757 she was consigned to the Marshalsea debtors' prison on the south bank of the Thames, but by December she had been released and was registering shares in a book called *The Servant's Directory*. In 1760 the last cookbook in Hannah Glasse's name was published; *The Compleat Confectioner* was reprinted several times, though its true author was an obscure artisan named Edward Lambert. Mrs. Glasse died at age sixty-two in September 1770.

Hannah Glasse had published her masterwork when she was thirty-nine years old and somewhere along the way she must have learned to cook. Did she have her former self in mind in her dedication: "this BOOK is only designed to INSTRUCT the Young and Ignorant"? By this time she had certainly become mistress of a wide repertoire as proclaimed in the subtitle to *The Art of Cookery*: "which far exceeds any thing of the kind yet published." Compiled is an apt term for the contents of *The Art of Cookery* as Mrs. Glasse does not hesitate to borrow from other works, though she craftily would change the titles of the recipes.

In those early days of copyright law (a definitive English act was passed in 1709), recipes were considered as "made by transcription," i.e., copied out one from the other. This is certainly true in *The Art of Cookery.* Cookbook plagiarism had continued unabated, and research by Jennifer Stead and Priscilla Bain has revealed that a third of the 972 recipes in *The Art of Cookery* was taken word for word from an anonymous work, *The Whole Duty of a Woman* (1737). At this time such plagiarism was common practice and indeed approved—it was an author's duty to pass on the finest recipes, with no insistence on originality. When later a certain Ann Cook in *Professed Cookery* (1760, 3rd ed) complained of Mrs. Glasse—"She steals from ev'ry Author to her Book, Infamously branding the pillag'd Cook, With Trick, Booby, Juggler, Legerdemain . . ."—no one else took much notice.

Always the canny saleswoman, Mrs. Glasse lists all her chapters on the title page of *The Art of Cookery*, opening prosaically with plain roasts and vegetable cookery and moving on to techniques such as To ragoo a Piece of Beef and dishes like Mutton Chops in Disguise (cooked in buttered paper), and ducks "dressed with onions, green peas, or cucumbers." The style of the recipes themselves differs little from Mrs. Woolley nearly a century before her, though Hannah Glasse is perhaps more conscientious in mentioning all the necessary ingredients, sometimes with quantities, and more or less in order of appearance. Chapter III brings a dig: "Read this chapter, and you will find how expensive a French Cook's Sauce Is," trumpets Mrs. Glasse, betraying her rooted prejudice against the French cuisine that held center stage on many fashionable tables. Elsewhere she exclaims, "So much is the blind Folly of this Age, that they would rather be impos'd on by a French booby, than give Encouragement to a good English Cook!" This remark can also be taken as a bid for feminism, as the vast majority of cooks following the French style were male. "Should I be so happy as to gain the good Opinion of my own Sex I desire no more," sums up Hannah Glasse to her readers.

Her huge chapter (more than three hundred recipes) on cooking a

Fast-Dinner is something of a catchall, perhaps designed as lighter fare to appeal to busy women as well as to cater the usual fish-on-Friday meals and Lenten dinners. The motley collection reminds me of the fare at my Cheltenham Ladies' Boarding School, where a starch was the foundation of every meal and pudding was the highlight of the day. At first glance Hannah Glasse does not appear to have a sweet tooth, and her two short chapters On Making Cakes and Of Cheesecakes, Creams, Jellies, Whip Syllabubs, &c. Sweets are modest compared with most cookbooks by women. It is reassuring to find that she has not forgotten the sweet puddings and pies—Orange Pudding, Pearl Barley Pudding, Apple Dumplings, Cherry Pie, and the like—they are hidden under For a Fast-Dinner. The short chapter For Captains of Ships may have had a personal link as Hannah's son, George Buck, was lost at sea when his Royal Navy ship sank in a storm on New Year's Day off Pondicherry, India.

Perhaps Mrs. Glasse's most remarkable recipe is Yorkshire Christmas Pie, harking back to the legendary medieval *rôti sans pareil* in which a dozen or more birds were boned and stuffed one inside another, starting with a thrush enclosing an olive and ending with a peacock in full plumage. Hannah Glasses's much later version involves five different birds, including a turkey, a goose, a chicken, a partridge, and a squab, baked in a raised pie crust made with melted butter. The finished pie is a masterpiece, a specialty of northern England where Mrs. Glasse was raised. "There Pies are often send to London in a Box as Presents," she remarks, "therefore the Walls must be well built." (London was then a four-day journey by coach.) Individual pork pies were a feature of my childhood, the staple of the local butcher, and very good they were, too.

Further chapters in *The Art of Cookery* emphasize the wide scope expected of the accomplished housewife. She must oversee wine making and brewing, the baking of bread, the preserving and distilling, all the while marketing according to the seasons. Preserving in brine or in an acid, usually vinegar, was limited but was the most feasible method, as given the temperate, damp English climate, air-drying and even dry-salting could be unreliable. Four chilling little recipes close out the list of 972 recipes: Two are to "Cure for the bite of a mad dog," one "Receipt against the Plague," and a final "How to keep clear from Buggs."

Table settings in the eighteenth century continued as they are in Hannah Woolley's time, with all the dishes for dinner laid on the table at once, like our buffets. "And where is great Variety of Dishes and a large Table to cover, so there must be a Variety of Names for them," instructs Mrs. Glasse. Perhaps she even supplied written labels so everyone knew what they were eating, as seen at today's grand hotels. On more formal occasions, the number of diners dictated the number of dishes, eight dishes for eight, sixteen for sixteen and so on, though exact

AT HOME IN THE KITCHEN

Women have had many jobs in and around the kitchen. As mistress of the house, if she were lucky, she had a *nécessaire* hooked into her belt, a small collection of implements such as scissors, a notebook and pen, a pincushion, all hanging on chains or ribbons for easy access. In smaller houses she was probably also the cook, working alone, or backed up by a scullery maid, and an outdoor hand to help with heavy lifting, slaughtering of animals, and digging the garden if there was one. The lady of the house issued daily working instructions, set dishes on the table, welcomed guests for relaxation and exchange of gossip as well as food. In colonial America, where a single chamber housed everyone, and eating and sleeping took place not far from the hearth, the cook was truly in charge.

In prosperous England, the cook's domain would have included a pantry (from the French *pain* meaning "bread") and a larder (from *lard*, or "bacon"), both of them for stor-

proportions were rarely observed. Dishes would be placed in elaborate patterns on the table and designs were given in some contemporary cookbooks, indicating an almost mountainous range of dishes culminating in a central peak, often a silver epergne or tureen. Roasts were set at the end of the table to be carved by the host. During the meal, particularly at grand dinners, some of the dishes would be replaced by others, but still maintaining the pattern. This was called a "remove."

Living in London, the center for international trade, Mrs. Glasse

age of supplies. The cellar or butler's pantry housed bottles. If a cow was kept for milk, the cook would have overseen the dairymaid. The cook or mistress of the house might be in possession of a stillroom for the preparation of preserves, cosmetics, and medicinal potions, possibly even equipped with an actual still for the delicate process of distilling perfumes and alcohol. During the eighteenth century, the stillroom was also the place for brewing tea and coffee. All of these tasks might be discussed in cookbooks, often in a separate chapter.

would have been spoiled for ingredients. Imports such as turkey and potatoes from the New World had become commonplace, together with new varieties of peas and beans, and she mentions the so-called French bean, a large, flat, totally edible pod, sometimes called a string bean, which defines its major handicap. The English love affair with the potato was about to begin and Hannah Glasse includes three Potatoe Puddings and Potatoe Cakes, plus some optimistic instructions "To make Potatoes like a Collar of Veal or Mutton." She also gives simple instructions on how to broil, fry, and mash potatoes, showing how novel this vegetable was in many kitchens. They rapidly became cheap, too. I often had them twice a day in boarding school.

The Art of Cookery was one of the first cookbooks to be circulated in colonial America but was not independently printed there until 1805 when "a new edition with modern improvements" was sold in Alexandria and Fredericksburg, Virginia. The English editions were already in wide circulation, but this new American book had an appendix of twenty-nine recipes of which "perhaps eighteen could be said to be American," says culinary historian Karen Hess in her introduction to a 1997 facsimile of the original, published by Applewood Books in Bedford, Massachusetts. She goes on to say that Mrs. Glasse was particularly popular in the American South, probably influential in "any number of [today's] southern recipes for syrupy custardy puddings baked in crust that bake up surprisingly translucent, such as the generic orange and lemon puddings." Tomatoes, which came from America, made the English shy, as they are members of the deadly nightshade family, but they do, points out Hess, creep into the American edition of *The Art of Cookery* in a single recipe, To dress Haddock after the Spanish way.

Mrs. Glasse was by no means the first woman to write such a cookbook in English—Hannah Woolley was before her—but the beautiful design of the first edition of *The Art of Cookery Made Plain and Easy* and the range of the nearly one thousand recipes set the work apart. She was writing not for the rich, but for literate cooks and prosperous housewives of the day (she mentions "every servant who can but read will be capable of making a tollerable good Cook"). Her breezy style and almost encyclopedic knowledge found a ready market, and her circulation spread over two continents, lasting until the end of the eighteenth century, marking new ground for any cookbook.

The career of Hannah Glasse has a very modern feel. Her illegitimacy, her elopement, her commercial ventures, and multiple bankruptcies would have made prime fodder for today's tabloids. The variety of her endeavors—and the energy with which she pursued them—her dressmaking schemes and her connections with royalty leave one breathless. She was indeed, as commented the culinary biographer Alan Davidson, "an indomitable spirit," one who blazed the way for future generations of women cookbook writers.

A Green Peas-Soop

The Art of Cookery Made Plain and Easy, 1747

TAKE a Quart of old Green Peas, and boil them till they are quite tender as Pap, in a Quart of Water, then strain them through a Sieve, and boil a Quart of young Peas in that Water. In the meantime put the old Peas into a Sieve, pour half a Pound of melted Butter over them, and strain them through the Sieve with the Back of a Spoon, till you have got all the Pulp. When the young Peas are boiled enough, add the Pulp and Butter to the young Peas and Liquor; stir them together till they smooth, and season with Pepper and Salt. You may fry a French Role, and let it swim in the Dish. If you like it, boil a Bundle of Mint in the Peas.

BIG AND BABY GREEN PEA SOUP

In Hannah Glasse's time, when peas came directly from the garden, they would likely be a jumble of both tender green pea pods and fat pods with tough old peas inside. Even today, at the farmers' market, a bag of peas will include lots of sizes. Cooking times for big and baby peas are radically different and Hannah solves the problem by making a purée with the old peas, then adding the newer little ones as garnish. The contrast of the mature pea purée with the sweetness of the baby peas is stunning.

SERVES 3 TO 4

6 quarts/6 liters pea pods (about 4 pounds/1.8 kg)
1 quart/1 liter water
Salt and pepper
3 to 4 sprigs mint (optional)
2 sticks/1 cup/225 g butter
A long baguette roll, for croutons (optional)

1. Shell the peas into two bowls, placing the fat old peas in one bowl and the smaller new ones in the other. Discard the pods.

2. In a saucepan, bring the water to a boil with a little salt and pepper. Add the fat peas and mint (if using) and simmer until the peas are very tender, 15 to 20 minutes. Drain the peas, discarding the mint and reserving the water.

3. In a stand blender or with a handheld blender, purée the cooked peas. If making croutons, set aside about one-quarter of the butter, then dice the rest and add it to the pea purée. Work again with the blender until smooth.

4. Bring the reserved water back to a boil, add the new peas with a little salt and simmer until just tender, 3 to 5 minutes. Drain the peas, then stir into the pea and butter purée. Taste, adjust the seasoning, and set the soup aside.

5. If making croutons, cut the baguette roll diagonally into ½-inch/1 cm slices. In a skillet, melt the reserved butter over medium heat and fry the bread, turning once, until browned, 2 to 3 minutes total.

6. Warm the soup until very hot—do not let it boil or the butter will separate. If the soup does separate, particularly when reheating, it must be worked again with a blender. Taste the soup, adjust the seasoning, and serve with the croutons floating on top.

To make Force-Meat Balls

The Art of Cookery Made Plain and Easy, 1747

NOW you are to observe, that Force-Meat Balls are a great Addition to all Made-Dishes, made thus: Take Half a Pound of Veal, and Half a Pound of Sewet, cut fine, and beat in a Marble Mortar or Wooden Bowl; have a few Sweet Herbs shred fine, a little Mace dry'd and beat fine, a small Nutmeg grated, or Half a large one, a little Lemon-peel cut very fine a little Pepper and Salt, and the Yolks of two Eggs; mix all these well together, then roll them in little round Balls, and some in little long Balls; roll them in Flour, and fry them Brown. If they are for any Thing of White Sauce, put a little Water on in a Sauce-pan, and when the Water boils put them in, and let them boil for a few Minutes, but never fry them for White Sauce.

VEAL MEATBALLS

Hannah Glasse's name "Force-Meat Balls" comes from the French word *farce.* Farce is a stuffing, but as she remarks, this mixture is far more versatile than just a stuffing or foundation for meatballs. It can be shaped as little sausages or patties, it can be fried, simmered in stock or water, served plain or in a tomato sauce. Ground lean pork is a good substitute for the veal; suet is ground beef fat. Here I suggest browning the savory mixture as meatballs (so much easier than making sausages!) to serve hot with tomato sauce or at room temperature for cocktails with a sauce for dipping. Do not keep them waiting as they easily dry out.

MAKES 10 TO 12 MEATBALLS TO SERVE 3 TO 4

½ pound/225 g ground lean veal
½ pound/225 g ground beef fat (suet)

Grated zest of ½ lemon

2 teaspoons chopped fresh parsley

1 teaspoon chopped fresh thyme or sage

1 teaspoon chopped fresh oregano or savory

1 teaspoon salt, or to taste

1 teaspoon pepper

½ teaspoon ground mace

½ teaspoon ground nutmeg

2 egg yolks

2 to 3 tablespoons/22 to 30 g butter, for frying

3 to 4 tablespoons/22 to 30 g flour, more if needed

1. In a bowl, mix the veal and suet with your fingertips as though making pastry dough. Sprinkle with the grated lemon zest, parsley, thyme, oregano, salt, pepper, mace, and nutmeg. Mix gently, then stir in the egg yolks with a wooden spoon to bind the mixture. In a skillet, melt 1 tablespoon of the butter and fry a small piece of meat; taste and adjust the seasoning.

2. Spread the flour on a shallow tray. Fill a bowl with cold water and wet your hands. Pick up a generous tablespoonful of the meat mixture and roll gently between your hands to make a 1½-inch/4 cm ball. Drop the ball into the flour and toss with two forks until coated. Continue with the remaining mixture.

3. In the skillet, heat the remaining butter until it stops sputtering. Add the meatballs and cook over medium-high heat, turning often with the forks, until browned and thoroughly cooked, 5 to 6 minutes. Serve the meatballs as soon as possible, hot as an appetizer or entrée, or at room temperature on sticks for cocktails.

To Pot Salmon

The Art of Cookery Made Plain and Easy, 1747

T A K E a Piece of fresh Salmon, scale it, and wipe it clean (let your Piece, or Pieces, be as big as will lye cleverly in your Pot) season it with Jamaica Pepper, black Pepper, Mace and Cloves beat fine, mixed with Salt, a little Sal prunella beat fine, and rub the Bone with; season with a little of the Spice, pour clarified Butter over it, and bake it well; then take it out carefully, and lay it to drain; when cold, season it well, lay it in your Pot close, and cover it with clarified Butter as above.

Thus you may do Carp, Tench, Trout, and several sorts of fish.

POTTED SALMON

"Potting" is an English term for preserving meats and fish by thoroughly cooking them in fat, then sealing them so no air can penetrate. Butter must first be clarified to remove whey and other impurities. Jamaica pepper is allspice. Sal prunella is potassium nitrate and available online, but given modern refrigeration, it's not needed for the recipe. Serve the salmon in the pot, scooping it out with a spoon. It is perfect for cocktails or as an appetizer with a baguette or crackers.

SERVES 10 TO 15

4 sticks/2 cups/450 g butter, more if needed

1½ teaspoons salt

½ teaspoon ground allspice

½ teaspoon pepper

½ teaspoon ground mace

¼ teaspoon ground cloves

A 2-pound/900 g whole skinless salmon fillet
Five ¾-cup/175 ml jam jars with lids

1. To clarify the butter, melt the butter in a small, deep saucepan, skimming any froth from the surface. Let the butter cool to tepid, then pour off the clear butterfat, discarding the whey.

2. Heat the oven to 350°F/175°C and set a rack in the center.

3. In a small bowl, mix together the salt, allspice, pepper, mace, and cloves. Cut the salmon in half lengthwise and lay, head to tail, on parchment paper or foil. Sprinkle the salmon with the spice mixture, coating both sides and patting gently so it adheres to the fillets. Transfer the parchment paper with the salmon to a baking dish just large enough to fit the fillets. Pour over the clarified butter so the salmon is completely coated, then cover the baking dish with foil and bake until the salmon is tender and thoroughly cooked, 30 to 40 minutes.

4. Let the salmon cool to tepid, then tilt the dish and pour off the butter and cooking liquid into a bowl. Chill until the butter is set, then discard any liquid and remelt the butter.

5. Cut the salmon into 2-inch/5 cm squares and pack it in the jars, adding the melted butter as you go to eliminate air bubbles. (Slide a narrow knife down the sides of the jars to release any air bubbles that do form.) Cover the salmon completely with the butter to seal it. Seal the jars and refrigerate for at least 6 hours until set. Potted salmon keeps up to 1 month in the refrigerator.

To Stew a Turky, or Fowl, in Sellery-Sauce

The Art of Cookery Made Plain and Easy, 1747

You must judge according to the Largeness of your Turky or Fowls, what Sellery or Sauce you want. Take a large Fowl, put it into a Sauce-pan or a little Pot, and put to it one Quart of good Broth or Gravy, a Bunch of celery wash'd clean, and cut small, with some Mace, Cloves, Pepper, and Allspice, ty'd loose in a Muslin Rag; put in an Onion and a Sprig of Thyme; Let these stew softly till they are enough, then add a Piece of Butter roll'd in Flour; take up your Fowl, and pour the sauce over it. An Hour will do a large Fowl, or a small Turky; but a very large Turky will take two Hours to do it softly. If it is overdone or dry it is spoil'd; but you may be a Judge of that if you look at it now and then. Mind to take out the Onion, Thyme and Spice, before you send it to Table.

WHOLE TURKEY IN CELERY SAUCE

A large bird has long been the centerpiece for grand feasts, but in Hannah Glasse's time, the favored English peacocks and bustards (wild birds that live in grasslands) had largely disappeared. Their ceremonial place was taken by the turkey, which was brought to Europe via the Middle East by early American explorers.

This recipe is ideal for a small turkey. You can count on a pound of meat on the bone to serve one person. The celery is cut in sticks and simmered in a cheesecloth bag alongside the bird, so it can flavor the sauce and also be used as a garnish. I like to keep the green celery tops to decorate the platter when serving.

Be aware that not only does the turkey itself take about an hour and a half to cook, but then the bird must be set aside while the broth is reduced for a couple more hours. The wonderfully moist bird, glazed in a golden rich sauce, is well worth the wait. Besides, the bird can be cooked the day before, and reheated in the broth before making the sauce. Throughout cooking, the oven is left free for the multiple side dishes of a great festivity. Note that this recipe is absolutely valid for a large chicken. Baby potatoes or boiled rice are the best accompaniments for the rich sauce.

SERVES 10

A 10-pound/4.5 kg turkey, with giblets if possible
1 bunch celery (about 2 pounds/900 g)
1 onion, peeled and quartered
2 sprigs thyme
5 whole cloves
4 to 5 blades mace
1 teaspoon black peppercorns
1 teaspoon allspice berries
2 quarts/2 liters chicken stock, or more if needed
4 quarts/4 liters water, or more if needed
Salt and pepper

To thicken the sauce
1 stick/½ cup/110 g butter, at room temperature
½ cup/60 g flour
Cheesecloth

1. Set aside the giblets from the bird and wipe the inside with paper towels. Truss the bird so it holds its shape and put it breast up in a stockpot or large, deep saucepan.

2. Discard any tough stems from the celery, then trim the ribs, setting aside the green tops for garnish. Halve each rib lengthwise, then cut crosswise into 2-inch/5 cm sticks. Wrap the celery sticks in a doubled piece of cheesecloth, then tuck down beside the bird, along with the onion and giblets. Wrap the thyme, cloves, mace, pepper-

corns, and allspice in another doubled piece of cheesecloth and add to the pot.

3. Add the stock with enough water to cover the bird, then cover the pot with a lid. Bring to a boil and simmer, skimming often, for 30 minutes. Taste the stock, adding salt if necessary and more water as needed to keep the bird covered. Turn the bird so it's breast down and continue simmering, adding more water to keep it covered. Allow 10 minutes cooking time per pound, or about 1½ hours for a 10-pound/4.5 kg turkey.

4. After an hour, or when the celery is tender when pierced with a two-pronged fork, lift out the bag and set it aside. Continue simmering the turkey. It is done when the meat shrinks from the leg bones, the legs are pliable when you wiggle them, and no pink juices run out when a thigh is pierced with a two-pronged fork. Divide the bird in pieces—it will be falling off the bone—arrange on a platter and cover with foil to keep warm.

5. To start the sauce, strain the stock, then pour it back into the pot and boil until reduced to 5 to 6 cups/1.25 to 1.5 liters; this may take up to 2 hours. When the stock is nearly reduced, return the bag of celery to the pot to reheat. Once hot, place the bag beside the turkey to keep warm.

6. To thicken the sauce: In a small bowl, cream the room-temperature butter, then work in the flour with a fork until smooth. Drop pieces of this kneaded butter into the boiling stock, whisking so the butter melts and thickens the sauce evenly. Add enough kneaded butter to thicken the sauce to your liking. Taste and adjust the seasoning.

7. To serve, spoon a little sauce over the warm bird pieces. Remove the celery from the cheesecloth, then arrange it on the platter beside the turkey and garnish with the reserved green tops. Serve the remaining sauce separately.

To make Chocolate Cream

The Compleat Confectioner:
or, the Whole Art of Confectionary
Made Plain and Easy, 1760

Take a Quart of Cream, a Pint of white Wine, and a little Juice of Lemon; sweeten it very well lay in a Sprig of Rosemary, grate some Chocolate, and mix all together; stir them over the Fire till it is thick, and pour it into your Cups.

CHOCOLATE PUDDING WITH ROSEMARY

Spanish explorers brought cacao beans back from Mexico in the sixteenth century, and chocolate became so popular as a drink that the Catholic Church split in heated debate over whether drinking chocolate on a fast day constituted a mortal sin. Chocolate as a flavoring, however, did not catch on until much later and Hannah Glasse was one of the first English cooks to use it. Adding an herb rather than a spice like cinnamon seems strange to us, but chocolate blends remarkably well with the aromatic flavor of rosemary. Muscat stands out as the classic sweet white wine, and a modest nonvintage half-bottle does fine in this recipe—just a cup is needed, with leftovers for the cook!

SERVES 6 TO 8

1 cup/250 ml sweet white wine
Juice of ½ lemon
¾ cup/150 g sugar
2 cups/500 ml heavy cream
2 sprigs rosemary
¼ pound/110 g dark chocolate, grated
8 small mousse pots or stemmed glasses

1. In a heavy-bottomed saucepan, stir the sugar into the white wine and lemon juice and heat gently, until the sugar is dissolved, 2 to 3 minutes. Remove from the heat and stir in the cream with a wooden spoon—it will thicken slightly and be full of bubbles. Add the rosemary and chocolate and continue stirring over low heat until the chocolate melts.

2. Bring the chocolate cream to a boil and simmer until the mixture is the consistency of thick cream, 4 to 5 minutes. Remove from the heat and let cool slightly, then strain into the mousse pots or stemmed glasses and refrigerate until cold before serving. The chocolate creams will keep up to 24 hours covered in the refrigerator.

To make Syrup of Roses

The Art of Cookery Made Plain and Easy, 1747

INFUSE three Pounds of Damask-Rose leaves in a Gallon of warm Water, in a well glazed earthen Pot, with a narrow Mouth, for eight Hours, which stop so close, that none of the Virtue may exhale. When they have infused so long, heat the Water again, squeeze them out, and put in three Pounds more of Rose-leaves, to infuse for eight Hours more, then press them out very hard; then to every Quart of this Infusion, add four pounds of fine sugar, and boil it to a Syrup.

ROSE PETAL SYRUP

In the seventeenth-century English household, roses were the flavoring of choice for pastries, which were infused with petals (preferably of Damask roses) from the garden. Hannah Glasse gives three recipes, one for a Conserve of Red Roses, another for a Conserve of Hips, and this gold-tinted Syrup of Roses. Homemade rose water is astonishingly fragrant, and the roses must be highly perfumed, unlike many tight-budded commercial varieties. Use the syrup to flavor custards, to freeze as an exotic sorbet, or as a base for your next cocktail. This is a recipe for high summer when roses proliferate—the petals are very light, so you will need a large number!

MAKES ABOUT 2 CUPS/500 ML SYRUP

2 quarts/2 liters rose petals (about ¾ pound/330 g)
1 quart/1 liter water
1 cup/200 g sugar
Cheesecloth; 2-cup/500 ml bottle with a cork

1. Pack half the rose petals in a jar. Heat the water until warm to the touch and pour it into the jar. Cover tightly and leave at room temperature overnight.

2. Strain the rose water through a double layer of cheesecloth into a bowl, squeezing tightly to extract maximum fragrance from the petals. Pack the remaining rose petals into the jar, pour over the strained rose water, cover, and again leave at room temperature overnight.

3. Strain the rose water again. In a small saucepan, heat the rose water with the sugar over low heat until the sugar is dissolved. Boil until reduced to about 2 cups/500 ml of syrup, 15 to 20 minutes. Let cool, then strain into the bottle and seal tightly with the cork. Rose syrup will keep in a cool place up to 1 month; refrigeration is not needed.

AMELIA SIMMONS

(dates unknown)

The cover of a recent edition of
American Cookery shows a portrait reputed
to be the author Amelia Simmons.

RECIPES

Chapter 3

AMELIA SIMMONS

American Cookery

*The first cookbook written by an American
using American ingredients.*

Amelia Simmons appears out of nowhere. As the writer of the first American cookbook, she has no direct links to predecessors in print on either side of the Atlantic. She was a loner, an independent spirit who on the title page of *American Cookery* declares herself as "An Orphan." There is no evidence that she had access to any other printed cookbook, though copies of Hannah Glasse's *The Art of Cookery Made Plain and Easy* would have been in circulation in America at that time. *American Cookery* harks back to a simpler, more demanding time of subsistence, of living off the land and making do with what you had. Meat and poultry were luxuries, vegetables strictly seasonal, and even common spices like cinnamon were carefully hoarded. These restrictions take me back to my World War II–era childhood in rural Yorkshire.

The first clue to Mrs. Simmons's identity lies in her Preface: "many hints are suggested for the more general and universal knowledge of those females in this country, who by the loss of their parents, or other unfortunate circumstances, are reduced to the necessity of going into families in the line of domestics, or taking refuge with their friends or relations." She is surely referring to herself. Her education must have been modest—in an "Advertisement" at the end of the book, Mrs. Simmons states she has employed a copy editor: "The author of the American Cookery not having an education sufficient to prepare the work for the press . . ."

Amelia Simmons underestimates herself; she was a genuine pioneer. The key to the success of her book lies in a simple phrase on the title page: "Adapted to this country." Amelia Simmons led the way in using indigenous American foods. Corn cobs are her fuel for smoking bacon, she gives the first recipes in any cookbook for slapjacks, "johny" or hoe cake, and lists three versions of Indian pudding, all using cornmeal, an American staple that the English settlers found hard to like. Benjamin Franklin, writing in the London *Gazeteer* in 1766, declared: "Pray, let me, an American, inform the gentleman, who seems ignorant of the matter, that Indian corn, take it for all in all, is one of the most agreeable and wholesome grains in the world and that johny cake or hoe cake, hot from the fire, is better than a Yorkshire muffin."

Corn was not the only ingredient mentioned by Mrs. Simmons that was unfamiliar to colonial settlers in New England. Fat for making pastry is "shortening" because it made dough "short," or crumbling; biscuits have become "cookies" (from the Dutch *koekje*); and scones are called "biscuits." One of her game-changing innovations was the use of "pearl ash" as a leavener derived from potash. This opened the way to characteristic loaf breads and cakes with a much lighter texture than those from Europe, raised with yeast or simply with eggs. Pearl ash led to the cheaper, quickly made sweet breads and muffins raised with baking soda and baking powder that have become typical of American baking and favorites of mine.

Amelia Simmons's education may have been sketchy, but she employs a wide vocabulary and a pretty turn of phrase. She comments on apples: "There is not a single family but might set a tree in some otherwise useless spot, which might serve the two fold use of shade and fruit." And on roasting beef: "rare done is the healthiest and the taste of this age." Her advice on choosing cheese could hardly be bettered today: "the inside should be yellow, and flavored to your taste." How right she is, always ask for a tasting.

The first edition of *American Cookery* was printed in Hartford, Connecticut, in 1796 and, judging by her list of ingredients, Amelia Simmons must have been a local resident. On the title page she sets the scene, presenting, she says, "The Art of Dressing VIANDS, FISH, POULTRY and VEGETABLES." These sections reveal typical New England fish from freshwater perch and rainbow trout, to shad, lobster, oysters, flounder, bass, cod, haddock, and eel from the sea. Her vegetables are equally characteristic of a cool northeastern climate and she devotes a whole page to green and kidney beans, and green peas. Lettuce is referred to, but quite overwhelmed by a fine list of half a dozen kinds of cabbage, a far sturdier crop. She would have regarded lettuce as a trendy plaything of low nutritional value—Thomas Jefferson had brought more than twenty varieties back from his sojourn in Paris as ambassador to France in the late 1780s. Mrs. Simmons does not like Garlicks, which: "tho' used by the French, are better adapted to the uses of medicine than cookery."

Mrs. Simmons maintained a close watch on her vegetable garden. More than a page of text is devoted to growing, storing, and cooking potatoes, reflecting their staple role as an indigenous crop. Roots include carrots, onions, beets, parsnips, and sunchokes, a member of the sunflower family that is native to North America. (Their other name, Jerusalem artichoke, is a corruption of *gira sole*, which is Italian for sunflower and translates literally as "follows the sun.") Even closer to Amelia Simmons's heart, and to her kitchen door, seems to have been parsley. She offers an elaborate procedure for growing parsley in a cask, roots planted inside, green leaves poking through the sides to be snipped with scissors and given as a present to neighbors. In summer the cask should stand against a south-facing wall, she instructs, and in winter in the cellar.

Traditionally, the cook was in charge of the yard, which included raising the poultry and tending the herb garden. In addition to parsley she mentions summer savory as good in sausages and legs of pork; sage, "used in cheese and pork, but not generally approved"; and pennyroyal, "a high aromatic . . . thyme, is good in soups and stuffings. Sweet majoram, is used in Turkeys."

The heavier work, the digging and planting of roots, the pruning of fruit trees, was the responsibility of the gardener, and Mrs. Simmons would be accustomed to being consulted on what to plant and when to

gather the produce. She is knowledgeable, even authoritative, on growing fruits, mentioning three types of pears for different seasons as well
as red currants, black currants, and grapes, "which grow spontaneously
in every state in the union." These would have been the native Con-
cord and its cousins, which yield a heavy, foxy wine. No wonder a mild
beer made from spruce trees was the standard household beverage, and
a source of vitamin C to prevent scurvy in the winter months. Amelia
Simmons's recipe for Spruce Beer uses spruce tree fronds and molasses
brewed with a concoction called Emptins, made from starch, hops, and
boiling water.

Inside the modern kitchen, we take for granted a plentiful supply
of pots, and serving dishes, but such equipment was severely limited in
Amelia Simmons's time. If no pie pan was available, one way around
the problem was to create a pie shell of pastry, and she has a fine list of
savory suggestions, including A Stew Pie using a whole veal shoulder
layered with salt pork, and a Sea Pie of pigeons, turkey, veal, or mutton
layered with sliced pork, salt, pepper, and flour for thickening. (The
name indicates it was intended to last during a sea voyage.) Minced pies
are based both on calves' feet with apple, or tongue with apple, currants
and cinnamon. "As people differ in their tastes, they may alter to their
wishes," she opines.

As for puddings, a staple of all early New England menus, Mrs. Simmons gets quite carried away. She has no fewer than six rice puddings,
a handful of bread puddings, puddings made from all the common
ingredients such as potato, apple, carrot, squash, pumpkin, orange, and
lemon, and a luxurious Cream Almond Pudding involving a quart of
cream, eight egg yolks, almonds, rose water, mace, and nutmeg for flavoring, all boiled together in a cloth to be served warm with melted
butter and sugar. Other desserts such as fruit custards and syllabub
reveal an English influence. Three cornmeal puddings, one plain and
two sweetened with sugar or molasses, hide under the header of A Nice
Indian Pudding. Perhaps the cornmeal Johny [Journey] Cake or Indian
Slapjacks, both lightened with some wheat flour, were more popular.
This is the first use in any cookbook of cornmeal.

All good cooks have their repertoire of cakes, plain loaves for every day, quick muffins for unexpected visitors, and rich, festive cakes for special occasions, and Amelia Simmons is no exception. Cakes were of such importance in her kitchen that they are listed on the *American Cookery* title page in extra large type with the note "from the imperial plumb to plain cake." Among the recipes, an echo of England returns with Shrewsbury Cake (little cakes lightly baked), Queens Cake (more little cakes, these flavored with wine, rose water, and "spices to your taste"), and A Cheap Seed Cake with caraway seed and allspice. Five varieties of gingerbread must indicate its constant presence in the pantry. Her Election Cake is never to be forgotten, a massive creation calling for 30 quarts of flour, 10 pounds of butter, 14 pounds of sugar, 12 pounds of raisins, 3 dozen eggs, a pint of wine, a quart of brandy, and sundry spices. It must have required a baker's oven to bake it, and a crowd of appreciative friends to eat it up.

In chilly New England, the kitchen invariably was the center of the house. In the early days, it was the principal living room, where all could benefit from the warmth of the great fireplace whose flues also heated upper and adjacent rooms. The central fire was usually kept going constantly, and during the day one or two smaller fires would be kindled on each side to boil kettles of water for washing and cleaning. Controlling the heat was tricky, and cooks learned early which logs had a fierce heat that died quickly compared with those that were steady burning, sometimes through the night.

All but the most primitive kitchens were equipped with a crane, hinged to swing outward, from which pots and kettles could be suspended over the fire. Meat and fowl were skewered on a spit for roasting. For frying, Amelia Simmons would have used "spiders," pans or skillets with three feet to steady them in the hot ashes. The original Dutch ovens were also used for baking: The base and lid were thoroughly heated in front of the fire, then the pie, bread, or cake was put inside and the oven surrounded by glowing embers, often also spread in the indented lid. The basic loaves of wheat and rye bread that anchored the diet came, however, from the communal oven of the village baker.

American Cookery was such a success that editions popped up all over the northern states, in Albany, New York, in 1796, a second edition in

Hartford, Connecticut, in 1798, then Salem, Massachusetts, in 1804, Walpole, New Hampshire, in 1812, Brattleboro, Vermont, in 1814, Poughkeepsie, New York, in 1815, Windsor, Vermont, in 1816, and a final appearance in 1822 in New York City. The number of small printings illustrates the transport problems posed in early colonial territory where roads were sparse and geographical barriers many. Not surprisingly, each edition of *American Cookery* varied somewhat, with recipes added or omitted here and there. Some editors might adjust the text, for example substituting milk for cream, or changing cooking times.

American Cookery also illustrates a perennial problem for publishers: plagiarism. In Montpelier, Vermont, *The New-England Cookery* by Lucy Emerson appeared in 1808, and a glance at the first line: "BEEF. The large stall fed ox beef is the best . . ." reveals that much of the text is word for word the same as *American Cookery.* The capital letters are identical and even the errors that Mrs. Simmons corrected in a later edition are included. However Lucy Emerson added more than sixty new recipes with sections "Of Frying," "Of Broiling," and "Of Stewing," and she includes an index. In her preface Mrs. Emerson does have the grace to acknowledge an earlier source: "It is with diffidence that I come before the public as an Authoress, even to this little work; I have no pretensions to the originality of the whole of the receipts herein contained, it is due to those ladies who have gone before me." To further mitigate the injury, Amelia Simmons herself had been guilty of plagiarism when she borrowed recipes from *The Frugal Housewife* (1765) an English cookbook by Susannah Carter that had been reprinted in Boston with plates by Paul Revere.

American Cookery is the first cookbook written by an American, intended for American cooks to follow in her footsteps. It remains an enduring favorite, setting the scene for future generations of cooks throughout New England and beyond. Mrs. Simmons's bare-bones style is far less sophisticated than that of the first English printed cookbook by Hannah Woolley dating from well over a century earlier. Even so, in the fragile nation that was the new America, Amelia Simmons's recipes establish a domestic pattern of plain, nourishing household meals that extend beyond the modest background of its author and the kitchens in which she cooked. Her simple dishes based on local ingredients, often raised by the cook herself, are an inspiration far beyond her small post-colonial backyard.

THE COOK OUTDOORS

A working cook always had responsibilities outside the kitchen. She would be in charge of the poultry, if only a few hens for the production of eggs. A more sophisticated poultry yard included ducks (who need a pond to moisten their webbed feet) and probably a few geese. Turkeys, a native American bird, were tricky to raise, and guinea hens would escape to roost in the trees at night if not carefully monitored.

Another responsibility of the cook might be a small garden of herbs including parsley, thyme, at least a couple of varieties of mint, with rosemary, sage, possibly oregano, and a bay tree. If space permitted, a patch of ground might include a few lettuces, cabbages in the winter, and an apple and a pear tree. Any vegetables such as potatoes, pumpkins and squash, leeks, and onions would require more space and a strong back for the digging. The more the cook could produce at home, the better.

To pickle Cucumbers

American Cookery, 1796

Let your cucumbers be small fresh gathered, and free from spots; then make a pickle of salt and water, strong enough to bear an egg; boil the pickle and skim it well, and then pour it upon your cucumbers, and stive [immerse] them down for twenty four hours; then strain them out into a cullender, and dry them well with a cloth, and take the best white wine vinegar, with cloves, sliced mace, nutmeg, white peppercorns, long pepper, and races [roots] of ginger, (as much as you please) boil them up together, and then clap the cucumbers in, with a few vine leaves, and a little salt, and as soon as they begin to turn their colour. Put them into jars, stive them down close. And when cold, tie on a bladder and leather.

TRADITIONAL PICKLED CUCUMBERS

All early cookbooks contain a disproportionate number of pickles, desperately needed to enliven the restricted diet of winter months. Little cucumbers remain a favorite, bitter to the tongue when raw but mellowed by pickling. As Amelia Simmons instructs, be sure they are firm and of more or less equal size. You will need to soak the cucumbers in brine several hours ahead. Long peppers are a spice, available online, as are canned leaves of grape vines.

MAKES 1¼ QUARTS/1.25 LITERS PICKLES

3 cups/750 ml water

1 cup (about 10 ounces/300 g) coarse salt

10 baby cucumbers (about 2 pounds/900 g)

For the pickle juice
3 cups/750 ml white wine vinegar
3 or 4 (1-inch/2.5 cm) pieces fresh ginger, peeled and thickly sliced
3 or 4 whole long peppers
3 or 4 blades mace
½ teaspoon whole cloves
1 teaspoon white peppercorns
½ teaspoon salt
1 whole nutmeg
5 to 6 canned or jarred vine leaves
One 5-cup/1.25-liter airtight jar

1. In a small, deep saucepan, heat the water and salt, stirring until the salt is completely dissolved (it should be concentrated enough to float an egg). Bring the brine to a boil, then skim any froth. Remove from the heat and add the cucumbers. Top with a plate and a weight to ensure the cucumbers are completely submerged in brine. Leave at room temperature 4 to 5 hours so that the cucumbers soften slightly.

2. Sterilize the jar. Make the pickle juice: In a deep pot, stir together the vinegar, ginger, long peppers, mace, cloves, white peppercorns, and salt. Put the nutmeg in a plastic bag, crush it with a rolling pin, and add to the pickle juice. Bring to a boil and simmer 10 minutes.

3. Drain the cucumbers in a colander and dry them on paper towels. Immerse the cucumbers, along with the vine leaves, in the pickle juice and bring to a boil. Simmer until the cucumbers start to change color, 5 to 6 minutes.

4. Let cool 5 minutes, then drain the cucumbers, reserving the pickle juice and spices and discarding the vine leaves. Pack the cucumbers and the reserved spices in the jar. Pour the warm pickle juice over the cucumbers until they are completely covered. If the cucumbers are not covered, boil more vinegar and add to the jar. Seal the jar. The pickled cucumbers will keep up to 1 month in a cool, dark place; they need not be refrigerated. They are best after at least a week of pickling.

Indian Slapjack

American Cookery, 1796

One quart of milk, 1 pint of Indian meal, 4 eggs, 4 spoons of flour, little salt, beat together, baked on gridles, or fry in a dry pan, or baked in a pan which has been rub'd with suet, lard or butter.

CORN GRIDDLE CAKES

Corn, the staple grain of American Indians, took some getting used to for colonial cooks. It's almost without gluten, the basic fabric of yeast breads, so a whole new repertoire of flatbreads and pancakes had to be developed. Some of them called for "pearl ash," the forerunner of baking powder, but this recipe from Amelia Simmons is leavened only with eggs. Serve the cakes plain, perhaps with melted butter or sour cream, shredded pork, or with the classic maple syrup and crisp bacon on the side.

MAKES 20 (4-INCH/10 CM) CAKES

2 cups/330 g medium ground yellow or white cornmeal
½ cup/60 g flour
½ teaspoon salt
4 eggs
1 quart/1 liter milk
1 to 2 tablespoons lard or butter (optional)
Griddle or skillet

1. In a bowl, stir together the cornmeal, flour, and salt. Make a well in the center and add the eggs and 2 cups/500 ml of the milk. Stir the eggs and milk together with a whisk, gradually drawing in the cornmeal mixture to make a smooth batter. Stir in half of the remaining milk.

2. Heat a griddle or skillet until very hot—a drop or two of batter should sizzle at once. Pour in 2 to 3 tablespoons of batter for a trial cake. When the cake is set on top and browned on the underside, 2 to 3 minutes, flip and brown the other side, about 1 minute longer. If the cake is heavy and thick, thin the batter with some of the remaining milk. If the cakes stick, rub the griddle with a paper towel dipped in melted lard or butter.

3. Continue frying the cakes, adding a scant ¼ cup/60 ml of batter to make 4-inch/10 cm cakes. Stir the batter before each batch as it separates on standing. Pile the pancakes one on top of the other to keep them warm while frying the rest. Serve as soon as possible, while still warm.

A Rice Pudding. No. 3

American Cookery, 1796

8 spoons rice boiled in 2 quarts milk, when cooled add 8 eggs, 6 ounces butter, wine, sugar and spices, bake 2 hours.

SPICED RICE PUDDING

From the early eighteenth century, rice was grown in the southern colonies of America, forming part of the region's brisk trade with New England. Mrs. Simmons would have used round-grain rice, the best being known as "Carolina Golde." Rice pudding, sweetened with sugar, must have been a staple, as she lists no fewer than six recipes with varying quantities of eggs and butter.

Spices are a personal choice and I'm suggesting the classic trio of cinnamon, ginger, and allspice that were common at that time. Amelia Simmons remarks, "The mode of introducing the ingredients, is a material point; in all cases where eggs are mentioned it is understood to be well beat; whites and yolks and the spices, fine and fettled [mixed]." This rice pudding forms a delicious custard layer on top; it can be served plain, or with berries or a fruit compote.

SERVES 6 TO 8

1 cup/200 g round-grain rice

2 quarts/2 liters milk

8 eggs

1 cup/200 g sugar

½ cup/110 g butter, at room temperature, more for the dish

1 teaspoon ground cinnamon

1 teaspoon ground ginger

1 teaspoon ground allspice
½ cup/125 ml red or white wine
10-cup/2.5-liter deep baking dish

1. In a saucepan, simmer the rice in the milk until tender, stirring often, 15 to 20 minutes. Remove from the heat and let cool.

2. Heat the oven to 300°F/150°C and set a rack in the center. Butter the baking dish.

3. In a bowl, with an electric mixer, beat the eggs with the sugar until thick and light, 2 to 3 minutes. Beat in the room-temperature butter, along with the cinnamon, ginger, and allspice. Using a spoon, stir the egg mixture into the cooled milk and rice, followed by the wine.

4. Pour into the baking dish and bake until the pudding is set and the top is browned, 1¼ to 1½ hours. If the top browns too quickly, cover it with a baking sheet. Serve warm or at room temperature.

Raspberry Cream

American Cookery, 1796

Take a quart of thick sweet cream and boil it two or three wallops, then take it off the fire and strain some juices of raspberries into it to your taste, stir it a good while before you put your juice in, that it may be almost cold, when you put it to it, and afterwards stir it one way for almost a quarter of an hour; then sweeten it to your taste and when it is cold you may send it up.

SIMPLE RASPBERRY CREAM

It's a rare recipe that calls for just two ingredients, but this is a fine one, and goes well with a crisp cookie. Very rich cream is boiled—a "wallop" is surely one of those burping bubbles that suddenly bursts on the top of a near-boiling thick liquid—then stirred until cool.

SERVES 4 TO 6

1 quart/about 450 g raspberries
1 to 1½ tablespoons sugar (optional)
2 cups/500 ml crème fraîche or raw unpasteurized heavy cream
<u>6 stemmed glasses</u>

1. In a food processor, purée the raspberries, working them in two batches. To remove the seeds, push the raspberries through a coarse sieve into a bowl. Set the purée aside, sweetening with sugar if you wish; discard the seeds.

2. In a saucepan, bring the cream to a boil, stirring often. Let simmer for 1 minute, then leave to cool, continuing to stir often. When the

cream is at room temperature, stir in the raspberry purée—it will thicken the cream.

3. Spoon the raspberry cream into the stemmed glasses and serve chilled or at room temperature.

A Butter Drop

American Cookery, 1796

Four yolks, two whites, one pound flour, a quarter of a pound butter, one pound sugar, two spoons rose water a little mace, baked in tin pans

ROSE WATER BUTTER COOKIES

The title "A Butter Drop" could be almost anything, though the high sugar content in this recipe narrows the scope. However the instruction "baked in tin pans" strongly suggests a small cake or cookie, so I've opted for cookies. Ground nutmeg can be substituted for mace.

MAKES TWO DOZEN 3-INCH/7.5 CM COOKIES

1½ sticks/375 g butter, more for the pans and topping
5 cups/575 g flour, more for shaping the cookies
2¼ cups/450 g sugar
2 eggs
2 egg yolks
1 tablespoon rose water
1 teaspoon ground mace

1. Heat the oven to 400°F/200°C and set a rack in the center. Melt the butter and use some to brush the baking sheets, setting the rest aside. Sift the flour into a bowl and stir in half the sugar.

2. In a bowl, with an electric mixer, whisk the whole eggs and egg yolks at full speed with the remaining sugar until thick and light, 1 to 2 minutes. Stir in the rose water and mace and the remaining melted

butter, reserving 1 to 2 tablespoons. Add the flour in three batches to make a dough.

3. Turn the dough onto a floured work surface and shape it into a log. Divide the log into 4 portions and cut each portion into 6 pieces (a total of 24). Roll the pieces into balls and set 12 on each baking sheet. Flatten them to 3-inch/10 cm rounds with a fork dipped in the remaining melted butter. Brush them with any remaining butter.

4. Bake the cookies one sheet at a time until lightly browned, 15 to 18 minutes. Transfer them to a rack to cool and bake the second sheet. Serve the cookies warm if you like, or they can be kept in an airtight container for 24 hours.

MARIA RUNDELL

1745–1828

The cook plucks the goose lying on the
kitchen table, with other birds waiting for
their turn, in the 1816 edition of
A New System of Domestic Cookery.

RECIPES

An Excellent Hotch-Potch, page 82

Veal (or Chicken) and Parsley Pie, page 84

Potatoe Rolls, page 87

Tomata Sauce, for hot or cold Meats, page 90

Mushroom Ketchup, another way, page 92

Lamb Hodgepodge, page 82

Veal (or Chicken) and Green Parsley Pot Pie, page 84

Potato Yeast Rolls, page 87

Vinegar Tomato Sauce, page 90

Portobello Mushroom Ketchup, page 92

Chapter 4

MARIA RUNDELL

A New System of Domestic Cookery

*A confident English bestseller that launched
nineteenth-century cooking on both sides of the Atlantic.*

The simplicity of Amelia Simmons and her rustic book *American Cookery* is a world away from the competent authority of Maria Rundell, yet there are fewer than ten years between the publication of the two books. *American Cookery* had had no colonial forerunner, but Mrs. Rundell was preceded by an advance guard of English cooks, culminating with Hannah Glasse and *The Art of Cookery Made Plain and Easy* (1747). A unique approach separates Mrs. Rundell's *A New System of Domestic Cookery* from Mrs. Glasse, who had created a work of art as well as a manual for elegant entertaining. Mrs. Rundell's purpose is very different, reflecting the broader status and responsibilities of a housewife in the troubled times of the Napoleonic Wars and the American War of Independence. With scarcely a stretch of imagination she could have supported Women's Liberation.

Maria Eliza Ketelby Rundell was the only known child of Abel Ketelby, a barrister and Londoner in the midland county of Shropshire. She was raised in comfortable circumstances and married Thomas Rundell, a physician from Bath who probably was also a partner in a prominent jewelry and silversmith company in central London. Their household would have had several servants, including a cook, a parlor maid, a nursemaid for the children, and a footman for the heavy work. They might even have kept a carriage. Mrs. Rundell was writing in exactly the same decade as Jane Austen, so the descriptions of Bath in *Persuasion* would accurately evoke the lives of the Rundells, who spent a year or two in Swansea, the fashionable seaside town where Maria Eliza wrote *A New System of Domestic Cookery.* With all the hosting that went on in such resorts, snacks like the Potatoe Fritters and Cheesecakes listed in *A New System* must have been very much the order of the day.

Rundell's interests ranged far beyond the mere recording of useful dishes for the table. "The mistress of a family should always remember that the welfare and good management of the house depend on the eye of the superior; and consequently that nothing is too trifling for her notice, whereby waste may be avoided." So opens the book of household management compiled by Mrs. Rundell to guide her daughters (she had five daughters and three sons). She herself had been an only child and perhaps felt the urge to document her knowledge. *A New System of Domestic Cookery, Formed upon Principles of Economy and Adapted to the Use of Private Families* first appeared in London in 1806 under the byline By A Lady. She foreshadows the moral rectitude of the Victorian era. This first edition, based on Mrs. Rundell's handwritten household book, apparently had many errors, but her publisher, John Murray, a veteran of such authors as Jane Austen, Lord Byron, and Washington Irving, was intrigued.

Murray was a friend of the Rundell family and together he and Maria Eliza developed the expanded, corrected edition of 1807 that we all think of as the official *New System of Domestic Cookery.* By the edition of 1810, nine full-page plates had been added, with a frontispiece showing a pantry piled with game and meat on a table, the fish on the floor. How much of the easy, readable style of *New System* is due to John Murray we cannot know, but the book is remarkable for its fluency and accurate punctuation. The recipes are equally refined; they were overseen by Mrs. Rundell, and while she specifies quantities and detailed instructions for items such as cakes and pastries, she leaves more freewheeling dishes like soups and sauces to the inspiration of the cook.

She herself comments: "In the following, and indeed all other receipts, though the quantities may be as accurately set down as possible, yet much must be left to the discretion of the person who uses them. The different taste of people requires more or less of the flavour of spices, garlic, butter, &c. which can ever be directed by general rules."

The early nineteenth century sees the era of "gravy"—usually based on beef, sometimes on mutton, veal, or ham—that might be served on its own as a sauce or spiked with flavorings such as port, Madeira, lemon, onion, or shallot. Gravy might be poured into the popular meat pies to bolster the filling and help preserve it by sealing out air. Unthickened gravy, what we would call stock, was used as aspic to glaze centerpieces of whole fish, poultry, or meats that would anchor a grand buffet. Mrs. Rundell describes how to create "Jelly to cover cold Fish," flavoring it with "lemonpeel, white peppers, a stick of horseradish, and a little ham or gammon." She clarifies it with egg whites and strains it through a jelly bag to be sparkling clear, just as we do today.

The dishes of a dinner were still not served one by one, but arranged together in the center of the table (round or rectangular), the number of main dishes being dictated by the number of diners. In between would be set little "entremets" of pastries, salads, vegetables, jellies, and more. Family dinner would be just one course, but a party might have one or two "removes" where the main dishes, particularly roasts, were replaced to form a second course. After a final clearance, the table would be reset with dessert, an array of sweetmeats and fruits.

These customs were so thoroughly established that Mrs. Rundell does not mention them. She takes many culinary aspects for granted, above all the tastes of her very English audience. Her desserts, ices, and cakes are particularly typical, including Baked Gooseberry Pudding, Curd Puddings or Puffs, Lemon Syllabubs, An Excellent Trifle, Apple Fool, Common Bread Cake, Plain and very crisp Biscuit, and of course Plum Cake rich with currants, raisins, and almonds, raised with yeast and laced with wine and brandy; ironically it contains no plums, not even prunes.

The recipes in *New System of Domestic Cookery* might be routine, but the book broke new ground as the first comprehensive guide to running a prosperous household, with more than 750 recipes and also a twenty-page introduction on managing the kitchen and pantry. Subjects covered include: money and the need to track prices and expenditure with written receipts; loaves of bread must be counted and meat weighed on arrival from the butcher; an inventory should be kept of furniture, linen, and china. Pantries should be stocked with sugars ground to a powder ready for use, washed and dried currants (a favorite flavoring of the time), and spices already ground. Last but not least, Mrs. Rundell explains how to welcome unexpected guests for "in every house some preparation is necessary for accidental visitors."

Storage of ingredients was a major concern, particularly in summer. Most houses had a cellar where the temperature remained below 55°F/13°C and above freezing in winter. Bags of flour should be upended each week, and thoroughly shaken to discourage lumps says Mrs. Rundell. Soap (when made at home) is to be dried slowly so the cakes do not crack. When buying poultry in the market, the feathers should be set aside to stuff mattresses and cushions. Bread was costly at this time in the middle of the Napoleonic Wars, and Maria Rundell abhorred waste: "Rolls, muffins, or any sort of bread, may be made to taste new when two or three days old, by dipping it uncut in water, and baking afresh or toasting." (This old trick is surprisingly still successful.)

A well-run kitchen relied on seasonings developed by the cook such as Kitchen Pepper (a finely powdered mix of ginger, cinnamon, black pepper, nutmeg, allspice, cloves, and salt), portable soup (similar to today's meat glaze often given to its French name of demi-glace), and a variety of ketchups starting with mushroom and including a type of fish sauce. Rather to my surprise Mrs. Rundell uses soy sauce, brought in from Asia, as a flavoring. Hams and the indispensable bacon were salted, sometimes smoked, and hung to mature in a cool, airy loft. Supervised by the mistress of the house was a stillroom (originally containing a still to brew alcohol) for the making of tea and coffee, the simmering of preserves, and the brewing of beer and fruit wines such as gooseberry, elderberry, and damson plum. In London, where Mrs. Rundell lived, all such preparations could be purchased, but a dedicated cook preferred to oversee at least some of them at home, particularly when alcohol was involved.

Mrs. Rundell must have been a kind and equitable head of household and she is very aware of setting an example. "Some part of every person's fortune should be devoted to charity," she remarks. She published two other books, one entitled *Domestic Happiness* and the other *Letters to Two Absent Daughters*. In *New System* she comments: "To refuse countenance to the evil, is to encourage the good servant." She is mindful of outward appearances and of economy: "The manner of carving is not only a very essential knowledge in point of doing the honours of the table with grace, but makes a great difference in family consumption; [a lady] should not fail to acquaint herself with an attainment of which she must daily feel the want. . . ." As for the novice carver, "It is to be observed that a thin sharp carving knife, and with very little strength to the management of it, will cut deep thin slices."

In England *New System* extended to sixty-five editions in thirty-five years. In America, by the end of 1807 the book had been published in nine cities including Boston, New York, Philadelphia, and down to Charleston, South Carolina, continuing to expand to at least thirty-seven American editions. Any of today's authors would have been proud. *New System* was also published in German in 1841. Following the custom of the time, none of these editions revealed the identity of the Lady until after Mrs. Rundell's death in 1828 in Lausanne, where she likely had retired to enjoy the mild climate.

Maria Rundell was already sixty-one in 1806 when John Murray had suggested the title for *A New System of Domestic Cookery*. When, two years after publication, Murray sent her a £150 fee, she declared she had had no thought of remuneration. However, as the success of the book became clearer, the tone changed. In 1814 Mrs. Rundell accused Murray of neglecting the book; she went to vice-chancellor's court for a restraining order and thus began one of the most famous cookbook publishing disputes of all time.

In 1821, after a thorough rewrite of *New System*, Mrs. Rundell took her manuscript to Longman, a London publisher as prestigious as John Murray. Court injunctions forbidding publication flew right and left until the lord chancellor himself ordered the litigants to settle privately. In 1823 Murray agreed to pay Maria Rundell "the sum of two thousand and one hundred pounds of good and lawful money." Relations must have been strained to say the least. In today's dollars, this amounts to just shy of $100,000.

Mrs. Rundell takes the writing of cookbooks a major step forward in terms of coverage and organization. What makes Mrs. Rundell stand out is her recognition of the importance of kitchen management, of "econ-

---

THE INGREDIENT EXCHANGE

In 1492 Columbus traveled to the New World, and during the next century vast quantities of unfamiliar foods crossed the Atlantic in both directions. A first, universal success was chocolate, served from the 1670s onward as a drink in cof-feehouses. Chocolate as an ingredient in recipes came later, though Hannah Woolley in 1661 mentions a "chaculato" drink of claret wine thickened with egg yolks and sweetened with sugar. Mrs. Woolley also talks of turkey, a bird that came to Europe via the Middle East, hence its name, and quickly gained popularity as an imposing presence on a festive table. The many members of the capsicum family spread around the Mediterranean, particularly chiles, which were valued for their heat. (Until then in Europe, mustard and horseradish were the only common peppery condiments apart from expensive peppercorns from the Far East.)

Our familiar staples, potatoes and tomatoes, both members of the nightshade family, had a mixed reception in

---

omy" used in the broadest sense of sound finances backed by knowledge and practical expertise. Nor does she ignore the most important people in the kitchen, the cooks: "such as are honest, frugal, and attentive to their duties, should be liberally rewarded." She speaks at length of ingredients and their treatment in the kitchen with respect, almost affection. She must have been an excellent boss and she must surely have enjoyed her dinner as much as she did describing how to cook it.

Europe. Tomatoes were welcomed in the seventeenth century in Spain, then England, but not until the early 1800s in France. The potato was equally controversial, though more popular in the northern countries as a dietary alternative to grain. Already in 1747, Hannah Glasse had included three recipes using potato in *The Art of Cookery Made Plain and Easy*. On the other side of the Atlantic, early immigrants to North America encountered a problem when making bread. Corn (maize), the indigenous American grain, thrived and was cheap, however it had to be combined with other grains to avoid pellagra, a nasty disease of the skin and nerves. Amelia Simmons knew this (though probably not the underlying medical cause—maize's lack of niacin) and her corn breads such as Johny cake and Indian Slapjack also include wheat flour.

An Excellent Hotch-Potch

A New System of Domestic Cookery, 1810

Stew peas, lettuce, and onions, in a very little water with a beef or ham-bone. While these are doing, fry some mutton or lamb-steaks seasoned, of a nice brown; three quarters of an hour before dinner, put the steaks into a stew-pan, and the vegetables over them; stew them, and serve altogether in a tureen.

LAMB HODGEPODGE

Fresh green peas and baby lettuces share the same late-spring season, so they are often combined in recipes. In Maria Rundell's day, the best lamb was also limited to springtime and this hot pot of hers must have been a celebration of all three. You may need to order the bones from the butcher ahead of time.

SERVES 4 TO 6

1½ quarts/1.5 liters shelled fresh peas (about 2 pounds/900 g)
10 to 12 baby onions (about 1 pound/450 g), peeled
2 beef or ham bones, split
Salt and pepper
4 heads Bibb lettuce (about 2 pounds/900 g)
6 thick lamb steaks or chops (about ½ pound/225 g each)
2 tablespoons butter

1. Spread the peas in the bottom of a large, deep pot and push the onions and bones down to the bottom. Sprinkle with salt and pepper. Trim the Bibb lettuce, then quarter the heads and lay on top of the vegetables. Sprinkle with more salt and pepper, then add about ¾ inch/2 cm of water to the pot. Cover and simmer until the peas

are tender and the lettuce is wilted, 7 to 10 minutes. Transfer the vegetables, bones, and liquid to a bowl and set aside.

2. Season the lamb steaks with salt and pepper. Melt the butter in the same pot over medium heat and brown the steaks, 2 to 3 minutes. Turn and brown the other side, 1 to 2 minutes longer. Add the reserved vegetables, bones, and liquid on top, spreading out the lettuce. Bring to a simmer, then cover the pot and continue simmering until the lamb steaks are very tender, 1½ to 1¾ hours. The onions may fall apart. Taste the juices and adjust the seasoning. Discard the bones and serve the steaks and vegetables from the pot.

Veal (or Chicken) and Parsley Pie

A New System of Domestic Cookery, 1810

Cut some slices from the leg or neck of veal; if the leg, from about the knuckle. Season them with salt; scald some parsley that is picked from the stems, and squeeze it dry; cut it a little, and lay it at the bottom of the dish; then put the meat, and so on, in layers. Fill the dish with new milk, but not so high as to touch the crust. Cover it; and when baked, pour out a little of the milk, and put in half a pint of good scalded cream.

Chicken may be cut up, skinned, and made in the same way.

EXCELLENT SHORT CRUST

Into a pound of flour well dried, rub three ounces of butter so fine as not to be seen—into some cream put the yolks of two eggs, beaten, and mix into the above into a smooth paste; roll it thin, and bake it in a moderate oven.

VEAL (OR CHICKEN) AND GREEN PARSLEY POT PIE

Mrs. Rundell mentions only salt in this recipe, but I've made a very English addition of pepper, nutmeg, and a bit of ground ginger. In *A New System of Domestic Cookery*, she gives the cook a choice of pastry dough, offering several recipes, including puff pastry, a hot water dough for venison pie, a "potatoe paste," and the above "Excellent short Crust" from which I have omitted the sugar. If using chicken, look for boneless, skinless chicken breast.

SERVES 6 TO 8

For the pie dough

2 cups/250g flour, more for rolling

1 teaspoon salt

6 tablespoons/90 g butter, diced, more for the pan

2 egg yolks

½ cup/125 ml heavy cream, more if needed for the dough and for
glazing the pie

For the filling

1 medium bunch parsley (about ½ pound/225 g)

4 veal scallopini or chicken breasts (about 1 pound/450 g)

1½ teaspoons salt

1 teaspoon pepper

½ teaspoon ground ginger

¼ teaspoon ground nutmeg

¾ cup/175 ml milk

1 cup/250 ml heavy cream

9-inch/23 cm deep pie pan

1. Make the pie dough: Sift the flour into a bowl with the salt. Add the
   butter and toss with your fingers until coated. With your fingertips,
   rub the butter into the flour to form fine crumbs. In a small bowl,
   whisk together the egg yolks and cream until mixed, then stir into
   the flour. Continue mixing with your fingers to form coarse crumbs;
   if they are dry, add a little more cream. Press the crumbs together
   and work lightly to form a dough. Wrap loosely and refrigerate.

2. Make the filling: Bring a medium saucepan of water to a boil. Discard
   the parsley stems and drop the leaves into the boiling water. Bring
   just back to a boil, 1 to 2 minutes. Drain the sprigs and squeeze
   them dry in paper towels. Chop them coarsely.

3. To assemble the pie, butter the pie pan and spread some of the parsley on the bottom. If using chicken, butterfly the breasts. In a small
   bowl, mix together the salt, pepper, ginger, and nutmeg and sprinkle

on the veal or chicken. Lay the seasoned meat in the pan, sprinkling each layer with more parsley, and mounding it slightly in the center so as to support the crust. Pour the milk over the meat; it should not touch the crust.

4. Sprinkle a work surface lightly with flour and roll out the dough to a 10-inch/25 cm round (about ¼ inch/5 mm thick) and cover the pie filling, trimming and fluting the edge. Use the dough trimmings to make decorations for the top of the pie, brushing them with a little cream if needed to help them stick. Refrigerate the pie for 15 minutes or until the dough is firm.

5. Heat the oven to 400°F/200°C and set a rack low down.

6. Brush the surface of the pie with cream to glaze it. Poke holes in the center with scissors for ventilation. Place the pie on a baking sheet to catch any drips and bake until lightly browned, about 20 minutes. Reduce the temperature to 350°F/175°C and continue baking until the meat is tender, 1¼ to 1½ hours longer. Lift the crust up and poke the meat with a skewer to be sure it is tender and fully cooked.

7. When done, take the pie out of the oven and let cool 8 to 10 minutes. Meanwhile, scald the cream. Lift up the pie crust, then pour off and discard the liquid formed at the bottom of the pan. Pour the hot cream over the meat, tipping the pan so the cream spreads evenly, then replace the crust. Leave the pie to cool. Serve warm or at room temperature.

Potatoe Rolls

A New System of Domestic Cookery, 1810

Boil three pounds of potatoes, bruise and work them with two ounces of butter, and as much milk as will make them pass through a colander. Take half or three quarters of a pint of yeast, and a half a pint of warm water, mix with the potatoes, then pour the whole upon five pounds of flour, and add some salt. Knead it well: if not a proper consistence, put a little more milk and water warm; let it stand before the fire an hour to rise; work it well, and make into rolls. Bake about half an hour in an oven not quite as hot as for bread.

They eat well toasted and buttered.

POTATO YEAST ROLLS

The white tubers we call potatoes, which are not related to sweet potatoes, were regarded with suspicion when they were first imported into Europe from Colombia in the mid-sixteenth century. They were not embraced in France or Germany, but the English were more welcoming and by the early 1700s potatoes had become commonplace. In this recipe they add not only flavor, but also a light, even texture to the baked rolls. They are usually served on the side at dinner. As Mrs. Rundell remarks, these Potatoe Rolls toast particularly well if they are leftover.

MAKES SIXTEEN 4-INCH/10 CM ROLLS

2 medium baking potatoes (about 1 pound/450 g)

1½ tablespoons butter, diced

1¼ cups/300 ml warm milk, more if needed for the dough and for glazing the rolls

1 tablespoon/10 g active dry yeast

2 cups/500 ml warm water

10 cups/1.2 kg flour, more for kneading

2 teaspoons salt

1. Cut the unpeeled potatoes in pieces and put them in a large sauce-pan of cold water. Cover, bring to a boil, and simmer until the pota-toes are tender when pierced with the point of a knife, 10 to 12 minutes. Drain the potatoes and let cool, then peel them. Put the potatoes in a bowl and crush them with a potato masher. Work in the butter and about half the warm milk, just enough to make a pourable mixture. Sterilize the preserving jars.

2. Sprinkle the yeast over ½ cup/125 ml of the warm water and stir briefly, then leave until dissolved, about 5 minutes.

3. In a large bowl, stir together the flour and salt and make a well in the center. Pour in the potato mixture, along with the yeast mixture, and the remaining milk and warm water. Mix these ingredients with your hand—its warmth helps activate the yeast—gradually draw-ing in the flour to make a smooth dough. It should be soft but not sticky; work in more milk or flour if needed.

4. Turn the dough onto a generously floured work surface and knead it with both hands, pushing it away, gathering it up, turning and then pushing it away again. Add more flour if needed and work until the dough is elastic and peels easily from the work surface, about 5 minutes. (Alternatively, knead the dough for 2 to 3 minutes with the dough hook of a stand mixer.)

5. Shape the dough into a ball and transfer it to a large, oiled bowl, flipping it so the surface is lightly oiled all over. Cover the bowl with plastic wrap and leave in a warm place until the dough rises and almost doubles in bulk, about 1 hour.

6. Rub two baking sheets with oil. To shape the rolls, knock the air out of the dough by kneading it lightly on a generously floured work surface. Roll it with your hands to a log about 14 inches/35 cm long. With a knife, cut the log crosswise into 16 even portions. Flour both

the work surface and your hands. Hold your fingers loosely in a cage over a portion of the dough and rotate your hand so the dough spins to form a smooth ball. Transfer it to one of the baking sheets and shape the remaining balls in the same way. (Experienced cooks can spin two balls at a time, one with each hand.) Brush the rolls with milk to glaze them. Leave the rolls in a warm place to rise, 20 to 30 minutes.

7. Heat the oven to 400°F/200°C and set a rack low down.

8. When the rolls are risen, bake them until lightly browned, about 10 minutes. Reduce the temperature to 350°F/175°C and continue baking until the rolls are thoroughly browned and sound hollow when tapped on the bottom, 15 to 18 minutes longer. The rolls are best freshly baked and still warm.

Tomata Sauce, for hot or cold Meats

A New System of Domestic Cookery, 1810

Put tomatas, when perfectly ripe, into an earthen jar; and set it in an oven, when the bread is drawn, till they are quite soft; then separate the skins from the pulp; and mix this with capsicum-vinegar, and a few cloves of garlic pounded, which must both be proportioned to the quantity of fruit. Add some powdered ginger, and salt to your taste.

Some white-wine vinegar and Cayenne may be used instead of capsicum-vinegar. Keep the mixture in small wide-mouthed bottles, well corked, and in a dry cool place.

VINEGAR TOMATO SAUCE

Tomatoes were regarded with suspicion when they were brought to Europe from the New World. By the time Maria Rundell was writing in England, tomatoes were still quite new, but were welcomed under early names, such as love apple and golden apple. This recipe also calls for chile peppers or cayenne, which had been eagerly embraced as more pungent alternatives to the indigenous English mustard and horseradish. This is a light sauce, almost a juice; use it as a base for soups or other sauces, or as a dip for steamed shrimp.

MAKES 2 QUARTS/2 LITERS TOMATO SAUCE

5 pounds/2.25 kg tomatoes
½ cup/125 ml chile vinegar or white wine vinegar with a large pinch
   of cayenne pepper
5 cloves garlic, finely chopped
1 teaspoon ground ginger
1 teaspoon salt

<u>4-quart/4-liter casserole, preferably earthenware, with a lid;
preserving jars</u>

1. Heat the oven to 325°F/160°C and set a rack low down.

2. Pack the tomatoes in the casserole and cover with the lid. Bake until the tomatoes are collapsed and soft enough for the skins to be removed easily, 45 to 60 minutes.

3. Let the tomatoes cool to tepid, then lift them out and remove and discard the skins and cores. Cut them in half crosswise and squeeze the seeds into a sieve set over a bowl. Reserve the juice and tomato flesh and discard the seeds. Coarsely chop the tomato flesh as for salsa and put it in a large bowl.

4. Stir the strained juice into the tomato flesh. Stir in the vinegar, garlic, ginger, and salt. Taste the sauce and adjust the seasoning—it should have a good balance of sweet fruit, vinegar, and spices.

5. Ladle the sauce into preserving jars. Seal the jars and store in a cool place or the refrigerator for up to 1 month. Serve at room temperature, or, if serving hot, bring the sauce just to a simmer to keep the fresh taste.

Mushroom Ketchup, another way

A New System of Domestic Cookery, 1810

Take a stew-pan full of the large-flap mushrooms, that are not worm-eaten, and the skins and fringe of those you have pickled; throw a handful of salt among them, and set them by a slow fire; they will produce a great deal of liquor, which you must strain; and put to it four ounces of shalots, two cloves of garlic, a good deal of pepper, ginger, mace, cloves, and a few bayleaves—boil and skim very well. When cold, cork close. In two months boil it up again with a little fresh spice, and a stick of horse-radish, and it will then keep the year; which mushroom ketchup rarely does, if not boiled a second time.

PORTOBELLO MUSHROOM KETCHUP

Ketchup made at home, from big, flat dark mushrooms, was one of the first bottled condiments, the name coming from the Chinese *ketsiap*, meaning a fermented fish sauce. The intense, zesty flavor of the mushroom brew, akin to Worcestershire sauce, must have been a revelation to early-nineteenth-century cooks, who normally relied on vinegar, verjuice (sour grape juice), and the occasional citrus to add piquancy to their cooking. The ketchup will keep a month in a cool place; for longer storage, it should be boiled a second time. Use as a condiment for scrambled eggs, vegetables, fish and shellfish, or think of it for your next Bloody Mary.

MAKES ¾ CUP/175 ML KETCHUP

2 pounds/900 g flat or portobello mushrooms
¼ cup/60 g coarse salt
2 shallots, thinly sliced

2 cloves garlic, sliced

3 blades mace

2 or 3 bay leaves

1 tablespoon black peppercorns, crushed

1 teaspoon whole cloves

1 teaspoon ground ginger

1-cup/250 ml bottle with a cork

1. Brush any debris from the mushrooms with a dry sponge. Slice the mushroom stems and quarter the caps. Put them in a large, shallow saucepan. Stir in the salt, cover, and heat as gently as possible, stirring occasionally. After a few minutes, the juices will start to run. Keep cooking until all the juices are rendered, 1¼ to 1½ hours. Let cool to tepid, then strain the mushrooms in a sieve set over a bowl, pressing to extract as much juice as possible. Discard the mushroom solids.

2. Put the mushroom juice in a medium saucepan with the shallots, garlic, mace, bay leaves, peppercorns, cloves, and ginger. Cover and simmer over low heat to extract the flavor, skimming often, 20 to 25 minutes.

3. Let cool, then strain into the bottle and seal tightly with the cork. The mushroom ketchup will keep in a cool, dark place up to 1 month; refrigeration is not needed.

LYDIA CHILD

1802–1880

Lydia Child smiles as she reads a book outdoors—
perhaps it was a cookbook!

RECIPES

Chapter 5

LYDIA CHILD

The Frugal Housewife

*The first comprehensive American book
on household management, designed as a guide
for the domestic goddess.*

"Dedicated to those who are not ashamed of Economy," reads the subtitle
of Lydia Maria Child's first and only cookbook, published in 1829. *The
Frugal Housewife* was her fifth book, written quite literally as a potboiler
to rescue the debts of her idealistic husband, a Harvard graduate and a
proponent of the abolition of slavery. Today, Mrs. Child is first thought
of as a civil rights leader: She was an early supporter of Native American
rights during her time and firmly advocated for the abolition of slavery.
She later supported rights for women's education, women authors and
journalists, and freedom for women to hold what were then scandalously
liberal opinions. Her recipes are simple and successful.

Lydia Maria Francis was born in Medford, Massachusetts, on February 11, 1802. Her early education from 1814 to 1820 was at a local
academy, what could be called a dames' school. Her mother died in
1814, when Lydia was just twelve, and she was sent to live with an older
married sister, Mary Francis Preston, in a town called Norridgewock in
present-day Maine, where Americans and Native Americans lived side
by side. Her father, Convers Francis, sent her off to Mrs. Preston's as a
result of young Lydia's "increasing fondness for books." Here she stud-

ied to be a teacher and in 1822 moved back to Massachusetts. Later Lydia was vocal on the subject of keeping small children busy, perhaps influenced by her teaching and family experiences.

Lydia's older brother Convers, given the name of his father, became a clergyman and eventually a professor at Harvard Divinity School. At home Convers was a great influence on Lydia (called Maria by her family), encouraging her to study the heroic writers—such as Homer, Ben Jonson, John Milton, and Sir Walter Scott—who were fashionable at the time. Lydia's father, a Unitarian Christian, is mentioned as a baker, though this is presumably in a general sense of running a business rather than engaging in the day-to-day manual work of commercial baking. This seems to be the only connection in Mrs. Child's early life with cooking. However, the Francis household was comparatively modest, though middle class, and young Lydia would have shared backstairs life with the servants and been familiar with the kitchen. In her recipes there are also traces of skills picked up from the Native Americans in Maine.

The Frugal Housewife was published when Lydia Child was twenty-seven. She had already accumulated a wealth of domestic experience. She remarks, "the writer has no apology to offer for this cheap little book of economical hints, except her deep conviction that such a book is needed." The tone is almost evangelical, her introductory chapter is laced with admonitions such as, "The true economy of housekeeping is simply the art of gathering up all the fragments, so that nothing be lost. I mean fragments of time as well as materials. . . . Time is money." Or "No false pride, or foolish ambition to appear as well as others should ever induce a person to live one cent beyond the income of which he is certain." The mid-1800s were of course moralizing times, but Lydia seems to push the envelope, influenced perhaps by the instability of her husband.

The book itself, less than one hundred pages, is printed on modest stock with no pictures, not even the customary portrait of the author as frontispiece. Instead, diagrams of cuts for beef, veal, mutton, and pork are shown. The five-page index at the back leads to handy blank sheets for personal notes. She does not spare space to begin chapters on new pages and the chapter titles such as Odd Scraps for the Economical, Simple Remedies, Cheap Dye Stuffs, and Cheap Common Cooking emphasize her focus on thrift. "Run the heels of stockings faithfully; and mend thin places, as well as holes." The fewer than forty recipes described in the Cheap Common Cooking chapter consist mainly of general advice on subjects such as Asparagus or Pies. Listing mince pies, pumpkin, carrot, custard, cranberry pies, she observes "these are dear pies for they take an enormous amount of sugar." Under gooseberries she comments, "Always remember it is more easy to add seasoning than to diminish it."

Mrs. Child's recipe style is like that of a journalist standing in the kitchen and observing the scene. By this date her cooking equipment would certainly have included a raised stovetop, but she might also have had one of the splendid cast-iron ranges developed by Count Rumford, which had not only flat hotplates for simmering stews, but also an enclosed oven heated from the fire beside it. Mrs. Child is more moralist than cook, more an economist than a creator of delicious dinners. Her pages are sprinkled with such maxims as "Nothing is cheap that we do not want," side by side with tips on things like keeping flour cool in the summer (immerse a large stone in the center). Her ingredients are basic: dried beans and peas, "mince meat," salt fish and salt pork. All is begun from scratch, including a kind of sourdough starter called "emptins." Bread and beer are prepared within the house. She gives quantities inconsistently and cooking times are vague. But none of this matters.

The recipes themselves, though frugal, are simple and reliable classics that anyone can enjoy. And they are delicious. Her Baked Indian Pudding is a fresh take on a Thanksgiving standard (inspired no doubt by her familiarity with Native American kitchens) and her Lobster Salad with only two main ingredients shines as delightfully as her instructions for picking the most handsome lobster. What she brings most of all to the kitchen are theoretical comments, though to be told: "No directions about these things will supply the place of judgment and experience," is surely discouraging to the novice cook.

In 1828 Lydia married David Lee Child, a radical leader of abolitionism and Native American rights. David Child practiced law in Boston, serving in the state legislature and was at one stage the editor of the left-wing *Massachusetts Whig* journal. He introduced Lydia to the inner circle of social reformers including Ralph Waldo Emerson, Theodore Parker, and John Greenleaf Whittier, all supporters of the abolition of slavery. The marriage was close in many ways: The couple shared similar interests and friends, working together on many social and political causes. David, however, was unreliable, and in 1845 he even went to jail. Lydia must have been all too familiar with the hardscrabble realities of running a household on an inadequate income. The situation became so bad that in the mid-1840s she was forced to legally separate her finances from those of her husband. They lived apart for at least six years, but were together when he died in 1874. Mrs. Child outlived him, and she proved tireless up until her death in the autumn of 1880 in Wayland, Massachusetts.

Lydia Child was already well known as an author when *The Frugal Housewife* was published. Her intellectual interests were wide-reaching, beyond the domestic sphere. Her first book was called *Hobomok, a Tale of Early Times* (1824), a daring novel of a mixed-race marriage between a white woman and a Native American man that provoked a scandal and healthy book sales. Next came a historical account of events leading up to the Boston Tea Party, with the deliberately provocative title of *The Rebels; or, Boston before the Revolution* (1825). She wrote no fewer than twenty-six books, ranging from novels challenging the racial and religious intolerance of the time to histories such as *The History of the Condition of Women, in Various Ages and Nations*, two volumes that appeared in 1835 as part of the Ladies' Family Library. From the beginning she realized that books for children such as her three volumes of *Flowers for Children* (1844–1847) were a promising market. She launched *Juvenile Miscellany*, the first periodical in the United States just for children. Other works include books on Native American settlements, *The Mother's Book* on "the rearing of children," a series called the Ladies' Family Library that included biographies of Madame de Staël and Madame Roland, and *An Appeal in Favor of That Class of Americans Called Africans*, an antislavery tract that proved so contentious that

Lydia was forced to step down as editor of the *Miscellany*. She is perhaps best known as a poet, the author of the iconic verse so often recited at Christmas and once learned by heart in American elementary schools:

> *Over the river and through the wood,*
> *To grandfather's house we go;*
> *The horse knows the way*
> *To carry the sleigh*
> *Through the white and drifted snow.*

If she had had children she would have kept them firmly at work. She says, "A child of six years old can be made useful . . . children can very early be taught to take all the care of their own clothes. They can knit garters, suspenders, and stockings; they can make patchwork and braid straw; they can make mats for the tables, and mats for the floor; they can weed the garden, and pick cranberries from the meadow, to be carried to market." She admonishes to "begin early. It is a great deal better for the boys and girls on a farm to be picking blackberries at six cents a quart, than to be wearing out their clothes in useless play." How very Victorian to inculcate a sense of purpose and discipline so young! Today's urge to give the juvenile imagination free range would not hold up in Mrs. Child's home.

Lydia Child differs from earlier, more practical cookbook writers such as Amelia Simmons and Maria Rundell in that her world was not centered on home and family. Mrs. Child had an intellectual grasp of how to run a household, in particular a kitchen. She had no children and few close relations. She was an independent woman whose scope ranged from the great ideological debates of the day to lightweight, sometimes scandalous novels. In *The Frugal Housewife*, she focuses on the home, but she was never really of it, devoting her mind and energy to the political and social concerns of the day. She reached out to a wider, more educated readership than most cookbook authors, thus adding prestige to what had previously been thought of as a purely domestic field.

In *The Frugal Housewife* Mrs. Child was setting a high bar for her readers and she was surely aware of it. What was intended to be a simple household manuscript became the direct inspiration for legendary American cookbooks that followed, including Fannie Farmer's *Boston Cooking-School Cook Book.* By the time Mrs. Child died in 1880, cookbooks and household encyclopedias had gained a lasting respect and recognition. In our post–women's liberation world, she is a familiar figure, the activist female intellectual who rouses controversy whenever she puts words on paper. A century ago such temerity was unheard of and Lydia Maria Child was a remarkably modern character.

Lobster Salad

The Frugal Housewife, 1829

The meat of one lobster is extracted from the shell, and cut up fine. Have fresh hard lettuce cut up very fine; mix it with the lobster. Make a dressing, in a deep plate, of the yolks of four eggs cut up, a gill of sweet oil, a gill of vinegar, half a gill of mustard, half a teaspoonful of cayenne, half a teaspoonful of salt; all mixed well together. To be prepared just before eaten. Chicken salad is prepared in the same way, only chicken is used instead of lobster, and celery instead of lettuce.

NEW ENGLAND LOBSTER SALAD

Lydia Maria Child's instructions on how to choose a lobster cannot be bettered: "A female lobster is not considered so good as a male. The female, the sides of the head, or what look like the cheeks, are much larger, and jut out more than those of the male, the mouth of a lobster is surrounded with what children call 'purses' edged with a little fringe. If you put your hand under these to raise it, and find it springs back hard and firm, it is a sign the lobster is fresh: if they move flabbily it is not a good omen."

The more freshly a lobster has been boiled, the more aromatic this salad will be—if possible, it should not be chilled.

SERVES 4

2-pound/900 g clawed lobster, boiled

4 hard-boiled egg yolks

2 tablespoons mild or Dijon mustard

½ teaspoon salt

¼ teaspoon cayenne pepper, more for sprinkling

⅓ cup/75 ml vegetable oil

⅓ cup/75 ml white wine vinegar

½ head iceberg lettuce (about ¾ pound/330 g)

1. Detach the lobster claws, then crack the claws with a nutcracker or hammer and extract the claw meat; set it aside. With your hands, pull the lobster tail in its shell from the body. With scissors, snip the underside of the lobster shell on each side and pull out the tail meat. Cut the meat in small chunks and put it in a bowl. Coarsely chop the claw meat and add it to the bowl. Using a large knife, cut the lobster body lengthwise in half and discard the head sac. Scrape the meat from the body, along with any coral (the orange eggs of the female), and add it to the bowl.

2. To make the dressing, work the hard-boiled egg yolks through a coarse sieve into a small bowl. Stir in the mustard, salt, and cayenne. Whisk the oil into the yolk mixture, followed by the vinegar. Taste the dressing—the flavor should be quite aggressive—and adjust the seasoning.

3. Shred the lettuce and toss it with the lobster meat. Pour the dressing on top, toss, and taste again for seasoning. Pile the salad on individual plates, sprinkle with a little cayenne for color, and serve.

Baked Indian Pudding

The Frugal Housewife, 1829

INDIAN pudding is good baked. Scald a quart of milk (skimmed milk will do) and stir in seven table spoonful's of sifted Indian meal, a tea-spoonful of salt, a tea-cupful of molasses, and a great spoonful of ginger, or sifted cinnamon. Baked three or four hours. If you want whey, you must be sure and pour in a little cold milk, after it is all mixed.

THANKSGIVING PUDDING

Corn, the staple grain of the Native Americans, was a challenge for early American cooks. It lacks the gluten found in wheat, which meant yeast could not be combined with corn to make bread. Puddings were the answer, whether savory or sweetened, usually with molasses. Grits or polenta are probably the nearest modern equivalent of the coarse, stone-ground meal used by Mrs. Child, and they create a sweet and savory side dish that is perfect for Thanksgiving.

For a softer pudding, before serving, heat 1 cup/250 ml milk and pour it over the pudding. This loosens the crispy crust that forms on the bottom. When the pudding has cooled slightly, it can be cut into squares.

SERVES 6

Butter for the baking dish
1 quart/1 liter milk
¾ cup/150 g coarse yellow or white cornmeal
⅓ cup/75 ml dark molasses
2 teaspoons ground ginger or cinnamon
1 teaspoon salt
9 x 7-inch/23 x 18 cm deep baking dish

1. Heat the oven to 350°F/175°C and set a rack low down. Butter the baking dish.

2. In a saucepan, bring the milk to a boil. Remove from the heat and stir in the cornmeal, molasses, ginger, and salt. Pour the mixture into the baking dish and bake for 30 minutes. Stir once, then continue baking until the pudding is set and starts to pull from the sides of the dish, 45 to 60 minutes longer.

Bird's Nest Pudding

The Frugal Housewife, 1829

If you wish to make what is called "bird's nest puddings," prepare your custard,—take eight or ten pleasant apples, pare them, and dig out the core, but leave them whole, set them in a pudding dish, pour your custard over them, and bake them about thirty minutes.

BIRD'S NEST APPLE PUDDING

The apples for this pudding should hold their shape during baking; Jonathan or Winesap are good varieties to use. A round baking dish is appropriate to mimic a pond, with the apple "birds" perched in a "nest" of baked custard. The custard is leavened only with eggs, as this recipe is early for the use of baking powder.

SERVES 4 TO 6

Butter for the pie pan
6 medium baking apples (2 to 3 pounds/900 g to 1.35 kg)
Brown sugar (optional)

For the custard
2 cups/500 ml milk
4 eggs, separated
½ cup/100 g granulated sugar
1 cup/125 g flour
1 cup/250 ml heavy cream, more for serving
1 teaspoon ground nutmeg
9½-inch/24 cm deep pie pan or round baking dish

1. Heat the oven to 350°F/175°C and set a rack low down. Butter the pie pan.

2. Peel the apples, then core them with an apple corer or a vegetable peeler. Set the whole apples in the pie pan, spreading them out, so they don't quite touch each other. If the apples are tart, sprinkle them with brown sugar. Bake for about 10 minutes.

3. Meanwhile, make the custard: In a small saucepan, scald the milk and set aside to cool. In a bowl, whisk the egg yolks with the granulated sugar until thick and light, about 1 minute. Stir in the flour, followed by the cooled milk. In a separate bowl, stiffly whip the egg whites, then fold them into the egg yolk mixture. Stir in the cream and nutmeg.

4. Pour the custard around the partly cooked apples and continue baking for 1 hour, then rotate the pan 180 degrees and continue baking until the custard is set and browned and the apples are tender, 15 to 20 minutes longer. Serve hot, while still puffed high, and with more cream on the side if you like.

Cranberry Pie

The Frugal Housewife, 1829

Cranberry pies need very little spice. A little nutmeg, or cinnamon, improves them. They need a great deal of sweetening. It is well to stew the sweetening with them; at least a part of it. It is easy to add if you find them too sour for your taste. When cranberries are strained, and added to about their own weight in sugar, they make very delicious tarts. No upper crust.

PIE CRUST

To make pie crust for common use, a quarter of a pound of butter is enough for a half pound of flour. Take out about a quarter part of the flour you intend to use, and lay it aside. Into the remainder of the flour rub butter thoroughly with your hands, until it is so short that a handful of it clasped tight, will remain in a ball, without any tendency to fall in pieces. Then wet it with cold water, roll it out on a board, rub over the surface with flour, stick little lumps of butter all over it, sprinkle some flour over the butter, and roll the dough all up; flour the paste, and flour the rolling-pin; roll it lightly and quickly; flour it again; stick in bits of butter, do it up; flour the rolling-pin, and roll it quickly and lightly; and so on, till you have used up your butter.

Always roll from you. Pie crust should be made as cold as possible, and set in a cool place; but be careful it does not freeze. Do not use more flour than you can help in sprinkling and rolling. The paste should not be rolled out more than three times; if rolled too much, it will not be flaky.

CRANBERRY TARTLETS

Mrs. Child offers only one pie dough, a rich, flaky mix that is rolled and folded two or three times, with each layer being dotted with butter and sprinkled with flour on the work surface, a preparation known in England as rough puff pastry. This yields a firm dough that is relatively impervious to moisture, and perfect for juicy cranberries. The fruit has changed little since Lydia Child's time, it still falls quickly into a purée when cooked, and demands a "great deal of sweetening." The tartlets make a cheerful Thanksgiving side dish, arranged around the turkey, or can be served as dessert, with a pitcher of heavy cream as the perfect accompaniment.

MAKES SIXTEEN 3-INCH/7.5 CM OPEN TARTLETS

For the rough puff pastry
4 cups/500 g flour, more for rolling
2 teaspoons salt
1 cup/225 g cold butter, cut in small dice, more for the molds/tins
¾ cup/175 ml water, or more if needed

For the filling
2 cups (¾ pound/325 g) cranberries
½ cup/125 ml water
½ cup/110 g brown sugar, or more if needed
½ teaspoon ground cinnamon or nutmeg
Sixteen 3-inch/7.5 cm tartlet molds or muffin tins;
    a 3½-inch/9 cm round fluted cookie cutter

1. Make the rough puff pastry: In a bowl, mix together the flour and salt. Add about one-quarter of the butter cubes and rub into the flour with your fingertips until it is so fine it sticks together when the crumbs are clamped in your fist. Work in the water and continue to work so the crumbs are damp and cling together to form a dough,

adding a spoonful or two more water if needed. Wrap loosely and refrigerate for 10 to 15 minutes.

2. Meanwhile, make the cranberry filling: In a small saucepan, combine the cranberries, water, brown sugar, and cinnamon and stir over medium heat until most of the cranberries have popped and the brown sugar is dissolved, 10 to 12 minutes. Set aside to cool. Taste and add more sugar if needed.

3. Sprinkle a work surface generously with flour and roll the dough to a rectangle about 6 inches/15 cm wide and three times as long. Dot half the remaining butter over two-thirds of the dough's surface. Fold the dough in three overlapping layers to form a square with butter between the layers. Seal the edges by pressing down with a rolling pin, then turn the package so the seam is facing you. Generously flour the work surface and repeat the rolling and folding process to add the remaining butter. Wrap and refrigerate the dough for 10 to 15 minutes.

4. To shape the tartlets, butter the tartlet molds or the cups of the muffin tins. Sprinkle the work surface lightly with flour and roll the dough to ⅛-inch/3 mm thickness, then stamp out 16 rounds with the 3½-inch/9 cm fluted cookie cutter and line the molds or muffin cups. Spread a heaping tablespoon of filling in each tartlet and refrigerate until firm, 10 to 15 minutes.

5. Heat the oven to 400°F/200°C and set a rack low down.

6. Place the tartlets on a baking sheet and bake until firm and lightly browned, 20 to 25 minutes. Let cool to tepid, then transfer to a rack to cool completely. Serve the same day, preferably freshly baked.

SARAH RUTLEDGE

1782–1855

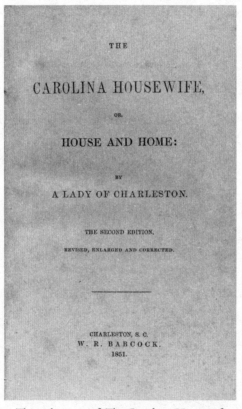

THE

CAROLINA HOUSEWIFE,

OR,

HOUSE AND HOME:

BY

A LADY OF CHARLESTON.

THE SECOND EDITION,

REVISED, ENLARGED AND CORRECTED.

CHARLESTON, S. C.
W. R. BABCOCK.
1851.

The title page of *The Carolina Housewife*
does not mention the author's name;
Mrs. Rutledge was a lady of stature
and kept her identity under wraps.

RECIPES

Chapter 6

SARAH RUTLEDGE

The Carolina Housewife

*A regional cookbook that reveals the secrets
of an aristocrat's Southern table, setting a new standard
of excellence for many cooks to follow.*

As a cookbook author, Sarah Rutledge is almost as far removed from her American predecessors, Amelia Simmons and Lydia Child, as can be imagined. They were both New Englanders and accustomed to standing in person at the stove. Mrs. Simmons picked up what education she had on the fly and was one of the few of her generation who earned enough by writing about cooking to lift themselves into the upper middle class. Lydia Child headed a modest, intellectual household. Sarah Rutledge was a Southerner, born with a head start and kin to American aristocracy—her father, Edward Rutledge, was the youngest signer of the Declaration of Independence.

An influential politician, Edward Rutledge was one of South Carolina's earliest governors and had married Henrietta Middleton, the daughter of a plantation owner. Henrietta brought to the marriage a property of more than six hundred acres, a vast expanse dedicated to the cultivation of rice. She would have been trained in the household management of a great plantation—the entertaining, the menus, the cooking, and indeed the finances. Together the Rutledges owned more than fifty slaves. Their family was small. Sarah (often called Sally and named for her Irish grandmother) was their only daughter, born in 1782, and she had two brothers, Henry Middleton Rutledge and Edward, who possibly died young. Her mother died when Sally was ten, but her father married again just six months later. The plantation tradition of hospitality can hardly have been interrupted in their home.

The Rutledges would have spent much of the year not on their plantations, but in their mansion in downtown Charleston. (The Middleton family plantation has been preserved as an American National Historic Landmark, open to the public.) By 1847, when Sarah Rutledge published *The Carolina Housewife*, her only book, she could look back on a lifetime as doyenne of Southern society, featuring rounds of spring presentation parties and languid summer suppers giving way to the festivities of Thanksgiving and the winter holiday season. When she set up house independently in Charleston, she would have been served by slaves. In her preface, Mrs. Rutledge declares "a house is not a home, though inhabited, unless there preside over its daily meals a spirit of order, and a certain knowledge of the manner in which food is to be prepared and served." Her advice when "company is suddenly brought home, by that notoriously thoughtless person, the husband," is to present "a clean table-cloth and a smiling countenance." Given this attitude perhaps it is no surprise that she herself never married—the title of Mrs. Rutledge is an honorary one.

Mrs. Rutledge describes simple, appetizing dishes sometimes as brief as three lines long. Her more than 550 recipes may be short, but she contrives to include information needed by an experienced cook, such as "do not boil after adding the cream." "Cut the fish into slices about an inch thick" runs a recipe for Drum Steaks, "Butter them and sprinkle over them a little wheat flour, pepper and salt. Fry of a rich brown in a pan." This tells all to the trained cook, with no further details of quantity or technique required. Or her Cheese Pudding, which is in effect a soufflé: "As soon as the mixture has risen well, and of a good colour, serve it immediately," she directs. Like other cookbook authors of this time, Mrs. Rutledge assumes the reader is able to supply such details as the heat of the oven, and the length of cooking times.

Sarah Rutledge would have had access to any foods that money could buy, but her palette of ingredients is not adventurous—she is writing for Carolinian cooks and she likes to stay local. Among half a dozen seafood dishes, turtle steaks stand out, and oysters were clearly plentiful to judge by the generous handful of recipes she accords them. Domestic poultry was not lacking when a household had a backyard, and passenger pigeons migrating in spring and fall provided a welcome interlude—a plump young pigeon makes good eating. Tomatoes, a New World vegetable absent from earlier European cookbooks, are thoroughly utilized by Mrs. Rutledge, with eleven recipes, including remarks on Cooking Tomatoes and Tomatoes for Winter Use. She was up to date with contemporary technology, using pearl ash (the forerunner of baking powder) and salaeratus, or baking soda, to vary the traditional yeast for raising breads. Her ices, which must have been sought after in that stifling summer climate, are a familiar run from almond to blackberry sorbet, with a sidestep into Matrimony, a happy union of fresh peaches macerated in sugar, enriched with heavy cream or custard.

Like many cookbooks of the time, *The Carolina Housewife* relies much on puddings, which range from Fancy Pudding, made of French bread spiced with cinnamon and served with a sugar, wine, and nutmeg sauce, to plain Fig Pudding and of course a range of rice puddings. Some require molds or baking dishes, but simpler ideas would have employed a stout unbleached cloth lined into a deep bowl, then filled with all manner of mixtures from Boiled Irish Potato Pudding to sweet Bread Pudding. Sarah Rutledge's entrée recipes reflect the tastes of the original English settlers with sauces such as gravy, white sauce, Bread Sauce or Oyster Sauce for Boiled Fowl or Turkey, and White Sauce for Cold Veal, Lamb, or Chicken. There is scarcely a trace of France beyond a "Ragout" here or an "a la Mode" there (no accents), let alone mention of Italy or Spain.

Given the surrounding monoculture, it is logical that *The Carolina Housewife* includes more than fifty rice recipes. The dozen rice breads are more like close-textured cakes than the spongy yeast breads of New England made with wheat flour. (Rice contains no gluten and so a batter or dough based on rice cannot be leavened with yeast.) In some of these breads, as well as in her soups, Mrs. Rutledge cooks her rice to a soft pulp to use as a thickener instead of wheat flour. She runs the gamut of Rice Slap-jacks, Rice Crumpets, Rice-drops, Rice Griddles, Soft Rice Cakes, Rice Biscuits, and many more that surely were inspired by her cooks. Savory rice-based dishes are surprisingly few, just a French pilau and a Carolina pilau, both featuring fowls (i.e., elderly chickens), with the Carolina version fragrant with bacon.

Rice was not just the staple crop of the surrounding plantations, it formed part of the foundational diet of the slaves who made the whole economy possible. Mrs. Rutledge's cooks would almost certainly have been black. Corn, the principal Native American grain, is also much used in *The Carolina Housewife*, in the form of meal in breads, biscuits, corn cakes, muffins, and wafers, with hominy appearing in spoon bread, breakfast cakes, and fritters. "In this work are to be found nearly 100 dishes in which rice or corn form a part of the ingredients," she declares in her preface. The Native American population is represented by a sprinkling of recipes such as Seminole Soup based on squirrel with hickory nuts and "a spoonful of parched and powdered sassafras leaves—or the tender top of a pine tree, which gives a very aromatic flavor to the soup." Mrs. Rutledge clearly welcomed these local dishes on her table, and, while she might have been appropriating them, we all benefit from their preservation. More than anyone among the twelve cooks described in this book, Mrs. Rutledge is an echo of a bygone age, a time when women cookbook writers were not in the kitchen themselves, but with their friends in the parlor while their servants presided at the stove.

The Carolina Housewife, published more than fifty years after Amelia Simmons's *American Cookery*, stands out among a new genre of cookbooks in America—regional works that highlight the distinctive styles of cooking that had developed in the various states. They are not manuals of household economy like Lydia Child's *The Frugal Housewife*. Instead, they document the foods and lifestyles of the local inhabitants and the dishes they ate. To this day, these early regional cookbooks remain an inspiration for modern cooks. It is no accident that many have been reprinted in facsimile, as they are for everyday use as well as for study as historical documents. Amelia Simmons unwittingly led the way with *American Cookery*, documenting the cooking of New England, much of which remains unaltered to this day. The cooking of Virginia was honored in *The Virginia Housewife* (1824), with foods from farther west appearing in 1841's *The Kentucky Housewife*. Mrs. Rutledge outlined the path of cooking in Charleston and the surrounding state. Her rice breads and the corn cakes are still prepared, as are the pickled shrimp and the peach preserves.

The Carolina Housewife makes no mention of budget nor of the practical operation of the kitchen. This contrasts with Mrs. Rutledge's near contemporary Lydia Maria Child, whose *The Frugal Housewife* is more of a tract in praise of household economy than a guide to entertaining. Mrs. Rutledge had no such worries, her arena was social, and in her preface she modestly acknowledges that the book is "a selection from the family receipt books of friends and acquaintances who have kindly placed their manuscripts at the disposal of the editor." All these contributions would undoubtedly have relied on her family and friends' slave labor. Perhaps it was these friends who persuaded Mrs. Rutledge, at the age of sixty-five, to publish *The Carolina Housewife*. Given her extensive social connections, she would have had a built-in market. A facsimile of this first edition of 221 pages was reprinted by the University of South Carolina Press, opening with an admirable introduction written in 1979 by Anna Wells Rutledge, a descendant of Sarah Rutledge's family.

The facsimile edition also includes a checklist of the forty-five South Carolina cookbooks published before 1935, all of them "direct descendants" of *The Carolina Housewife*. Anna remarks that "the earliest known private recipe books are family affairs, handed down from woman to woman, but the first published cookbooks are by men of considerable social standing. When women begin to publish their own cookbooks, they remain modestly anonymous, no South Carolina woman being named on a title page until the twentieth century." This included Sarah Rutledge, whose name is not mentioned in early editions of *The Carolina Housewife*.

Charleston lies at the heart of the fertile Low Country and *The Carolina Housewife* embodies that heritage. Part of the cookbook's fascination is the picture it paints of the mid-nineteenth-century South, the bustle of business, a flowering of fashion and entertainment, and a society rich in wealth and culture. Mrs. Rutledge passed her last years with her cousin and lifelong friend Harriott Pinckney, dying in Charleston in 1855, six years before the Civil War swept away the prosperity she brought to life so vividly in *The Carolina Housewife*. Nonetheless the book has proved to be a leader of the American genre of regional cookbooks that continues to flourish. Fannie Farmer, writing a generation later in New England, must have been very much aware of this regional cookbook tradition. Miss Farmer was writing for a very different, more educational purpose, but like Mrs. Rutledge, she was a stout proponent of writing recipes with the reader clearly in mind.

Chickens a la Tartare

The Carolina Housewife, 1847

Cut a fowl in pieces, and fry it brown. Cut a large onion, and also fry that brown; add three pints of good veal sauce, a little lemon-juice, a little turmeric, and season to your taste.

GOLDEN CHICKEN

This two-sentence recipe gives little hint of its stellar quality. The name given by Mrs. Rutledge has no connection with our modern use of "tartare," meaning raw. Instead, at its heart, it is one of the classic "mother" sauces, a velouté based on veal stock that is thickened with a butter and flour roux, and made golden with turmeric and a bit more lemon juice than usual. Boiled rice—rice is still grown in the Carolinas—is the perfect accompaniment. If you are using commercial chicken stock for the sauce, I suggest you opt for half stock, half water.

SERVES 4 TO 6

6- to 8-pounds/2.7 to 3.6 kg chicken, cut into eight pieces
Salt and pepper
2 tablespoons butter
1 large onion, chopped
2 teaspoons ground turmeric

For the velouté sauce
1½ sticks/170 g butter
¾ cup/100 g flour
6 cups/1.5 liters veal stock, or more if needed
Juice of 1 lemon, or more if needed
Salt and pepper

1. Trim the backbone and any flaps of skin from the chicken pieces, then sprinkle the chicken with salt and pepper. In a large skillet, melt the butter over medium heat and when it stops sputtering, add the chicken, skin side down. Continue cooking briskly until the skin is well browned, 8 to 10 minutes, then turn and brown the other side, 5 to 6 minutes longer.

2. Meanwhile, make the velouté sauce: In a large saucepan, melt the butter, then whisk in the flour and cook until starting to brown, 1 to 2 minutes. Whisk in the veal stock and bring to a boil, stirring until the sauce thickens. Add the lemon juice and simmer 1 to 2 minutes, then taste and adjust the seasoning—it should be quite piquant with lemon. Set the sauce aside.

3. Take the chicken pieces from the skillet and set them aside. Add the onion to the skillet, sprinkle with salt and pepper and fry, stirring often, until golden brown, 5 to 7 minutes. Stir in the turmeric and cook, stirring, until fragrant, about 1 minute. Stir in 2 to 3 cups/500 to 750 ml of the velouté sauce and mix well. Stir this onion and turmeric sauce into the remaining velouté sauce, taste and adjust the seasoning.

4. Push the chicken pieces down into the velouté sauce. Cover and simmer over low heat until the chicken is very tender when pierced with a two-pronged fork, 1 to 1½ hours. Some pieces, including the drumsticks and wings, will cook before others. If the sauce gets too thick, add a little more veal stock. The chicken and sauce can be cooked up to 24 hours ahead; cool completely, then cover and refrigerate.

5. For serving, warm the chicken over low heat until it is very hot, 8 to 12 minutes. Taste and adjust the seasoning. Transfer to a platter and coat the chicken pieces with sauce, serving the rest separately.

Zephyrinas

The Carolina Housewife, 1847

Mix a pint of flour with a small spoonful of butter; add sufficient water to make a dough that may be kneaded, and some salt. When sufficiently kneaded, roll very thin—not thicker, if possible, than a sheet of paper—cut with a saucer, prick with a fork, and put in an oven moderately warm. They are baked almost instantaneously.

ZEPHYR WAFERS

A zephyr is the lightest of west winds, embodied in these ethereal wafers, which are even lighter than the South's famous beaten biscuit crackers. They are perfect with cheese or with dips.

MAKES 25 TO 30 WAFERS

2½ cups/300 g flour, more if needed
½ teaspoon salt
2 tablespoons butter, cut into dice, more for baking sheets
¾ cup/175 ml water
3½-inch/9 cm round cookie cutter

1. Put the flour in a bowl and sprinkle over the salt. Add the butter and mix with your fingertips until it is evenly distributed. Sprinkle the water over the flour and continue mixing, pulling apart the stringy crumbs that form. Press the dough together in a ball. If it seems sticky, work in more flour. Knead the dough on a floured work surface until smooth but not elastic, about 1 minute. When the dough is the right consistency, it peels easily from the work surface in one piece. Transfer the dough to a bowl, cover with plastic wrap, and leave for at least 1 hour to allow the gluten in the flour to relax.

2. Heat the oven to 425°F/220°C and set a rack low down. Butter two baking sheets.

3. On a clean work surface, roll the dough as thinly as possible, less than $\frac{1}{16}$ inch/2 mm thick; it will not stick and no flour should be needed. Cut as many 3½-inch/9 cm rounds as possible using the cookie cutter or with a saucer as a guide. Roll each round individually until paper-thin and about 4 inches/10 cm in diameter. Set the rounds on the baking sheets. Gather the scraps and roll again to make more rounds.

4. Prick the rounds all over with a fork, then bake until crisp and very lightly browned, 6 to 8 minutes. Watch the wafers carefully, as they scorch very easily during the last minute of baking. Serve as soon as possible.

Sugar Ginger Bread

The Carolina Housewife, 1847

Two pound of flour, one and a half pounds of sugar (brown), one pound of butter, nine eggs, one cup of powdered ginger, and a cup of wine; rub the butter and sugar to a cream; beat the eggs and add them; stir in the flour, ginger, and wine.

BLOND GINGERBREAD

Sarah Rutledge must have dearly loved the taste of ginger. Among her recipes, she includes five different ginger cakes, four gingerbreads, and a sweet corn bread flavored with ginger and molasses. Looking at proportions, her teacups would have been smaller than our 8-ounce measuring cups, and here I have halved her recipe. She uses the classic method for mixing pound cake, which yields a blond, crumbly gingerbread, inviting a dollop of whipped cream or a side of fresh berries.

MAKES A RECTANGULAR BREAD TO SERVE 10 TO 12

3½ cups/450 g flour, more for rolling
3 tablespoons ground ginger
2 sticks/225 g butter, more for the pan
1⅔ cups/330 g brown sugar
4 eggs
3 tablespoons white wine
9 x 13-inch/23 x 33 cm rectangular pan

1. Heat the oven to 350°F/175°C and set a rack low down. Generously butter the pan, then line the bottom with a sheet of parchment paper and butter the paper.

2. Sift the flour with the ginger.

3. With an electric mixer or by hand, cream the butter, then beat in the brown sugar and continue beating until very soft and light, 3 to 5 minutes. Add the eggs, one by one, beating well after each addition. If the mixture separates slightly after the last egg (it will look curdled), beat in 2 to 3 tablespoons of flour. Divide the flour into three batches and stir in one at a time, adding the wine before the last batch of flour.

4. Transfer the batter to the pan and smooth the top with a spatula. Tap the pan on the counter to eliminate any air bubbles. Bake until the gingerbread is risen and firm in the center, 35 to 45 minutes. It should be lightly browned and pulling away from the sides of the pan.

5. Transfer the bread to a rack to cool. It is good as soon as it is baked, or it can be unmolded, tightly wrapped, and kept at room temperature up to 1 week; the flavor will mellow.

Regent's Punch

The Carolina Housewife, 1847

To two quarts of green tea, add half a pint of currant jelly, a little champagne, and the juice of four lemons; sweeten with loaf sugar, and add old spirits or brandy to your taste.

THE PRINCE REGENT'S PUNCH

This mildly alcoholic punch must have been named for the English Prince Regent, who employed the legendary chef Antonin Carême at his fantasy Pavilion in the beachside resort of Brighton. The mixture starts deceptively mild, with tea and "a little" Champagne, but calls for a kicker of "old spirits" (perhaps schnapps or gin) or brandy "to your taste." Mine led me to the following proportions. In winter, the punch is refreshing at room temperature; in summer, you could freeze a cup or two of the mixture as ice cubes.

MAKES 3½ QUARTS/3½ LITERS PUNCH
  TO SERVE 8 TO 10

1¼ cups/375 g red currant jelly
10 cups/2.5 liters brewed green tea, cooled
1 cup/250 ml Champagne or sparkling white wine, or to taste
Juice of 4 lemons (about ¾ cup/175 ml)
1 cup/250 ml Cognac, or to taste
Punch bowl

In a small saucepan, melt the red currant jelly in 1 cup/250 ml of the tea. Let cool, then pour into the punch bowl and stir in the remaining tea, along with the Champagne and lemon juice. Stir in the Cognac and taste, adding more Cognac or Champagne, if you wish.

FANNIE FARMER

1857–1915

True to form, Fannie Farmer holds up a standard cup
containing sugar, carefully measured and leveled
in the prescribed manner.

RECIPES
_____

Chapter 7

FANNIE FARMER

The Boston Cooking-School Cook Book

*The definitive guide to American cooking
with detailed ingredients and instructions that led
to the more systematic cookbooks of today.*

Fannie Farmer was a thoroughly modern woman. She made the modest Boston Cooking School famous, and with it *The Boston Cooking-School Cook Book*, developing a multifaceted business of teaching not just domestic cookery but offering classes for waitresses, even hospital nurses as well. She explored the role of diet and science in food, and she wrote a half-dozen bestselling cookbooks that set the scene for a generation to come. The American cookbook authors who precede Fannie Farmer are lightweights by comparison. The two regional books *The Virginia Housewife* and *The Carolina Housewife* feature fewer than two hundred recipes each, while in *The Frugal Housewife*, fellow Bostonian Lydia Maria Child gives fewer than forty cooking recipes scattered among her general culinary advice. Miss Farmer's subjects reflect the range of her career, from good family dinners to food science, catering, and cooking for the sick. Fannie pioneered the field in teaching young women to cook. She was a perfectionist, according to her cousin Wilma Lord Perkins, constantly asking "Could this be improved?"

Fannie is often referred to as Fannie Merritt Farmer, Merritt being her mother's family name. She was born in Boston in 1857, the eldest of the four daughters of John Franklin Farmer, "a stately man of great charm but little practical ability," commented Wilma. The Farmers were a close-knit family, warmhearted, and of "untainted New England stock, Unitarian and bookish." They lived in Medford, near Boston, and when in high school, Fannie hoped to go on to a college education. As the family expanded they moved back into the city in search of greater prosperity. However in her midteens Fannie was paralyzed by a seizure, remaining an invalid for several years and walking with a limp. This lessened her marriage prospects, the main path for a girl of the time, but Fannie was undeterred. She was determined to contribute to the family income, and in her twenties she recovered well enough to become a paid mother's helper to the Shaw family, who lived nearby.

Fannie continued to yearn for further education and in 1887, at the age of thirty, she enrolled in the Boston Cooking School for a two-year course. The school had been open for ten years and was considered a leader among several other Boston cooking schools. After graduation, Fannie stayed on as assistant to the principal, Carrie Dearborn, who was delicate in health and resigned two years later in 1893. The trustees then elected Miss Farmer as head of the school. At this time, Boston was led by a stronghold of Yankees who lived in Back Bay, a neighborhood of elegant brick row houses that overlooked the Charles River and housed an elite audience of young ladies who looked ahead to prosperous marriages and managing at least a servant or two. Under Fannie's business direction, the Boston Cooking School developed two streams of students: the young brides and older ladies who wished to instruct their cooks so as to improve dinners for their acquaintances, and the servants who prepared and served at such events.

Fannie proved an energetic and capable director, often found in the kitchen testing recipes and trying out new ideas. The story goes that it was a curious student who questioned the heaping tablespoons and cup measures that were customary. "Couldn't they be level?" she asked. Realizing the implications, Fannie instituted the custom of running the back of a knife across the top of the tablespoon or cup measures in her recipes, earning her the nickname "Mother of Level Measurement." "You should have in mind, too," she admonishes in *Catering for Special*

Occasions, "that in all these rules of mine the measurements are made level." Fannie also enjoys the science of cooking, writing with erudition on dextrose, starches, pasteurization, and albumins. This domestic science movement appealed to the next generation, with its rational approach to the art of cooking.

The Boston Cooking School had already inspired a cookbook, *Mrs. Lincoln's Boston Cook Book*, published in 1884 by Roberts Brothers and compiled by Mary Lincoln, an early teacher at the school. However this volume fell short of Fannie's high standards. Not only were there too few recipes to make it a comprehensive reference work, she felt the instructions were inadequate. Her nephew, Dexter Perkins, remembers Fannie limping up and down the room as she dictated her own manuscript to his mother. Photographs of Fannie show a high forehead and strong chin, her red hair piled high and lightening handsomely at the temples; her general expression is serious, though not without a glint of humor. Her students remembered her with lively affection as well as with respect.

In the kitchen Fannie usually wore a long white apron and white cap, the same attire as her students. However, family lore has it that the day she delivered her manuscript to a top Boston publisher, Little, Brown, she dressed with care including white gloves. She managed to sell and negotiate a contract for *The Boston Cooking-School Cook Book* herself. The hefty, brick-like shape of this first edition evokes the Victorian era. The book is neatly designed with clean open spacing of Miss Farmer's text, and recipes that invite notes from the cook (a few remarks in her own hand have survived in one modern facsimile edition). Advertisements for Knox gelatin and Hub ranges (among others), which helped finance the first edition, are confined to the back. The book was an instant success. The first edition of five thousand in 1896 was quickly followed by a second. No fool Fannie, she kept the copyright and when she died in 1915, more than half the value of her estate of $160,000 was in copyrights. *The Boston Cooking-School Cook Book* outsold all other American cookbooks of the nineteenth century, its success only checked in 1914 by the outbreak of World War I.

The Boston Cooking-School Cook Book belongs unmistakably to New England, as did its forerunner, Lydia Child's *The Frugal Housewife*.

There the resemblance ends. *The Frugal Housewife* was written to raise money for the family expenses, whereas *The Boston Cooking-School Cook Book* was founded on years of professional experience in the kitchen and had a built-in market of students at the school. Lydia's choice of recipes is haphazard, ranging from Calf's Head to Cider Cake. In contrast, Fannie's dishes—Yorkshire Pudding for Beef, Mint Sauce for Roast Lamb, Imperial Cake (harking back to the glories of Queen Victoria)—make clear the English heritage of the Yankee upper classes. French fare was now in style and Fannie includes recipes such as Consommé, Ramequins Soufflés, and Fish à la Provençale. There are almost no Southern flourishes of Virginia, nor tropical whiffs of Louisiana among the preponderance of white sauces and boiled squash.

Despite Boston being a major port, Fannie's section on fish is half that on beef and other meats. In her kitchen, bread is clearly not bought from a nearby baker, but made at home, varying from plain Water Bread through Boston Brown Bread to Parker House Rolls, named for a landmark Boston restaurant. She has fewer pickles and preserves than is commonly found in earlier cookbooks, reflecting a more plentiful supply of fresh ingredients. An array of sweet desserts and cakes are clearly intended for easy entertaining—Macaroon Cream (using granulated gelatin, a ready prepared product), a Thanksgiving Pudding based on crackers, and her famous Boston Cream Pie is not a pie at all but a relatively simple cake. There are few poultry recipes. Fannie was writing for an urban cook who might or might not be able to raise chickens in the backyard—raising poultry had long been the responsibility of the lady of the house. The alternative of buying chickens in the market must have been expensive but certainly saved time.

A major reason for the success of *The Boston Cooking-School Cook Book* is Fannie Farmer's skill in writing recipes. Reading them, it is clear that she herself has personally tested every one, adding remarks such as "During cooking, turn chicken frequently, that it may brown evenly" and in Escalloped Potatoes "add hot milk until it may be seen through top layer." She follows two formulas: For simple dishes, she buries the ingredients inside instructions such as those for Cream Whips: "Sweeten thin cream, flavor with vanilla, brandy, or wine, then whip:

half fill frappé glasses with any preserve, pile on lightly the whip." This cursive style had been traditional. It works very well for easy recipes that call for just a few ingredients. However for more complex dishes, the cook needs a clear head to disentangle ingredients from the running text. Here Fannie takes charge and lists exactly what is needed just below the title, thus also providing a shopping list. This practice opens the question "How much?" and Fannie answers this, too, thus developing the familiar recipe style we still follow now. Fannie Farmer may not have been the first to list ingredients at the head of recipes, but she led the way to its standardization. Less user-friendly are her many cross references that need looking up in the index, for example "Slice cabbage as for Cole Slaw," and "Mix as for Cream Filling I." Auguste Escoffier, who was Fannie's contemporary, follows the same habit in his *Guide Culinaire*, so perhaps this was the fashion of the day.

The Boston Cooking-School Cook Book is the most famous of Fannie Farmer's cookbooks, but she wrote several others, some with catchy titles such as *Chafing Dish Possibilities* (1898), *Catering for Special Occasions, with Menus and Recipes* (1911), and *A Book of Good Dinners for My Friends: Or "What to Have for Dinner"* (1914), which showcase Fannie's experience and expertise. Fannie kept up with medical ideas, seen in her *Food and Cookery for the Sick and Convalescent* (1904). In later years, Miss Farmer traveled a good deal, lecturing and teaching. She handed out printed recipes so that participants could focus on the action, rather than having to take notes.

Once she had the means to do so, Fannie enjoyed the delights of the table. She liked taking railroad trips with her family to New York to dine in such restaurants as Delmonico's, famous for its steak, the Astor, the Knickerbocker, and the fashionable Waldorf-Astoria. The midnineteenth-century emphasis on strict economy in household management was dissolving in the optimism of the Gilded Age, and, as a hub of trade, Boston was on the cutting edge. The pleasures of good living were more and more widely available: "In these days of rapid transit, by sea as well as by land, the markets of the world are brought almost to our very doors, and we have a hundred combinations to our grandmother's one," remarks Fannie in *Catering for Special Occasions*.

When interviewed in 1910, she explained to Jules Huret, a visitor from France, what her students learned in sixty lessons. "In the first course, we show them how to lay a fire, how to use a gas stove, how to cook potatoes and eggs and bake bread and apples, how to filter coffee, and how to make bread dough, simple soups and a few puddings." In later courses came pastries, salads, and desserts, together with serving instructions, table decorations, how to choose wine and liqueurs—all

WITHIN THE RANGE

Until the end of the seventeenth century, almost all domestic cooking took place over an open hearth. In fact a hundred years earlier the equivalent of today's stove burner had been invented, a raised cooktop fired by charcoal. It consisted of a hollow cube of fireproof bricks, topped by an iron grid with a charcoal fire beneath. However charcoal was an added expense and the toxic fumes needed to be ventilated, so a stove remained a luxury limited to kitchens with a window.

A breakthrough came with the development of cast-iron grates with metal "cheeks" to hold them in place over the coals. Finally the whole fire became enclosed and called a "range," with a flat top for heating pots and a ventilation chimney above. In America they were known as Rumford stoves, named for an engineer who pioneered cast-iron stoves in the late eighteenth century. The whole arrangement could be quite complicated with flues and dampers

the adjuncts to sophisticated dining. Fannie herself oversaw every aspect of the curriculum. "I saw these girls putting on the cap and apron as they arrived. They seemed to be having great fun playing housekeeper," reports Monsieur Huret.

By now, household management was a subject to be learned in school, not just picked up in a working kitchen, and *The Boston Cooking-School Cook Book* made this clear with sections on Ingredients, Cookery, and

to control the heat and doors to form ovens. To one side of the fire (usually a mixture of coal and wood) would be a hot water tank filled from above, with a side tap to draw out the heated water. The temperature of the top surface of a range would vary from searing hot in the center to a slow simmer at the edges. The descendants of these ranges are the Scandinavian-style models currently popular in England and other chilly climates, where they heat radiators and the bath water as well as ovens, stovetops, and the kitchen itself.

such subjects as How to Combine Ingredients, and Ways of Cooking. Scientific innovation was flourishing, the new kitchen stoves were powered by gas instead of dirty, back-breaking wood and coal. The two-handed egg beater was patented in 1884, saving the muscle-power demanded by a whisk (cakes using a dozen eggs were not uncommon, though it must be added that the eggs themselves were smaller than those today). According to the cookbook's advertisements, F. A. Walker & Co. could supply a variety of "choice house furnishings," including a meat grinder, a water bath full of little pots, and a chafing dish powered by some version of Sterno.

No wonder *The Boston Cooking-School Cook Book* was so successful—the 567 pages of the first edition cover almost every imaginable aspect of running a prosperous urban household in New England in the late nineteenth century. The book is almost the last of the great Victorian cookbooks, such as Catharine Beecher's *Miss Beecher's Domestic Receipt Book* (1846) and the English *The Book of Household Management* by Isabella Beeton (1861), a guide to a world that vanished in the onslaught of World War I. Miss Farmer herself exemplifies the confident energy of the latter half of the nineteenth century, and she goes further: She leads the way into the twentieth century, an era when more and more people of every class were starting to dine outside the home but also doing more of their own cooking. Active to the end, her last lecture was just ten days before she died, in 1915.

The Boston Cooking-School Cook Book has never gone out of print. By 1930 a million copies had been sold, rising to 2.5 million in 1947. By the mid-1960s, the power of personality had taken over and new editions of *The Boston Cooking-School Cook Book* began to include Fannie Farmer's name in the title, evolving to being simply titled *The Fannie Farmer Cookbook* for the last several decades. Food authority James Beard later remarked in the introduction to the thirteenth edition of *The Fannie Farmer Cookbook* (1979) that she must have had "a delicate and beautiful palate." Everyone who likes to cook has heard of Fannie Farmer. Over the years, the text has been revised and the recipes updated, but the essential Miss Farmer remains. As the "mother of level measurement" and more generally in leading the way to modern recipe writing, she is irreplaceable. Forthright and fluent, she expresses the spirit of her times and to this day her cookbook remains a valuable reference, an infallible guide to simple, everyday dishes. Her successor in the field of bestsellers, Irma Rombauer, brought a very different focus and spirit to culinary writing in *The Joy of Cooking*, but she respected the structure that had been masterfully established by Fannie Farmer.

English Monkey

Chafing Dish Possibilities, 1911

Soak one cup stale bread crumbs in one cup milk, fifteen minutes. Melt one tablespoon butter, add one-half cup soft, mild cheese cut in small pieces, and stir until cheese has melted; then add soaked crumbs, and just before serving, one egg, slightly beaten, one-half teaspoon salt, and a few grains cayenne. Pour over toasted crackers.

CHEESE AND CRACKERS

Fannie Farmer must have been inspired by "rarebit," the toasted cheese dish that is a longtime favorite in England. Here she thickens the melted cheese (she probably used white Cheddar from Vermont) with milk-soaked bread crumbs and pours it over crackers. The name of the recipe implies this is finger food, a forerunner of nachos. As a variation, you could add a slice of tomato under the cheese topping.

SERVES 2 TO 3

2 slices/90 g stale white bread
1 cup/250 ml milk
1 tablespoon butter
½ cup/60 g diced mild Cheddar cheese
Water crackers, for serving
1 egg, beaten to mix
½ teaspoon salt
¼ teaspoon cayenne pepper, more for sprinkling

1. Dice the bread slices, including the crusts, and freeze until firm, about 1 hour. In a food processor, work the diced bread to crumbs, 30 to 60 seconds. Soak the bread crumbs in the milk for 15 minutes.

2. In a small skillet, melt the butter, then add the cheddar and stir over low heat until melted, about 1 minute. Remove from the heat and stir in the soaked bread crumbs and milk.

3. To serve, spread the crackers on a serving dish. Heat the cheese mixture until very warm. Whisk in the egg, salt, and cayenne pepper. Continue whisking a few seconds over medium heat to cook the eggs and thicken the mixture. Pour the cheese mixture over the crackers, sprinkle with a little cayenne, and serve.

Fried Scallops

The Boston Cooking-School Cook Book, 1896

Clean one quart scallops, add one and one-half cups boiling water, and let stand two minutes; drain, and dry between towels. Season with salt and pepper, roll in fine cracker crumbs, dip in egg, again in crumbs, and fry two minutes in deep fat; then drain on brown paper.

CRISPY FRIED SCALLOPS

The larger the scallops, the better they are for breading and deep-frying. To plump them, Fannie Farmer soaks the scallops briefly in boiling water, then coats them in cracker crumbs and egg, yielding wonderfully crisp morsels to be eaten at once. She would probably have used beef tallow or lard for frying, but I suggest vegetable oil. As an accompaniment, I suspect Fannie would have served mashed potatoes, a very English side dish. She does not add a garnish, but a sprig or two of parsley or a very thin slice of lemon would not be amiss.

SERVES 4

½ pound/225 g water crackers (from about 15 crackers)
2 eggs
Salt and pepper
1½ pounds/675 g large scallops (12 to 16)
About 1 quart/1 liter very hot water
Vegetable oil, for deep-frying

1. Break the crackers in pieces and put them in a plastic bag. Pound with a rolling pin until very coarsely crushed, then spread on a tray. In a shallow bowl, whisk the eggs with a little salt and pepper.

2. Discard the small tough muscle at the side of each scallop. To plump them, put the scallops in a bowl, pour over the hot water, and leave for 2 minutes. Drain the scallops and place on paper towels, patting them dry.

3. Dip a scallop in the cracker crumbs, tossing with two forks until it is coated. Transfer the scallop to the egg mixture, turning until it is coated, then return it to the cracker crumbs and toss it again to form an even layer of crumbs. Set the cracker-coated scallop on a tray and coat the remaining scallops in the same way.

4. In a deep fryer or deep skillet, heat enough oil to cover the scallops. When the oil is hot enough for a drop or two of water to sputter, add 4 or 5 scallops and fry over medium-high heat until golden brown, 1 to 2 minutes, turning once. Remove the scallops and drain them on paper towels. Reheat the oil if necessary and fry the remaining scallops in batches.

5. Serve the scallops at once on individual plates.

Hot Slaw

The Boston Cooking-School Cook Book, 1896

Slice cabbage as for Cole-Slaw, using one-half cabbage. Heat in a dressing made of yolks of two eggs slightly beaten, one-fourth cup cold water, one tablespoon butter, one-fourth cup hot vinegar, and one-half teaspoon salt, stirred over hot water until thickened.

COLE-SLAW

Select a small, heavy cabbage, take off outside leaves, and cut in quarters; with a sharp knife slice very thinly. Soak in cold water until crisp, drain, dry between towels, and mix with Cream Salad Dressing.

WINTER COLESLAW

This hot slaw is a cold weather dish, good with roast pork or a festive bird. Poor Fannie Farmer had to revive faded winter cabbage in cold water, but ours can be relied on to be fresh and crisp. She does not specify what kind of vinegar is "hot," so I've opted for the mild bite of cider vinegar. This dish reheats well.

SERVES 4

½ small cabbage (about 1 pound/450 g)

For the dressing
2 egg yolks
¼ cup/60 ml water
¼ cup/60 ml cider vinegar, or more to taste

1 tablespoon butter, diced
½ teaspoon salt, or more to taste

1. Cut the cabbage into quarters, then cut out and discard the cores. Set the cabbage, flat side down, on the cutting board and slice it very thinly across the remaining cores, discarding any remaining thick bits of core. Transfer the cabbage to a sauté pan or other wide, shallow pan.

2. Make the dressing: In a double boiler or a heatproof bowl over a pan of simmering water, whisk together the egg yolks, water, vinegar, butter, and salt. Heat gently, whisking constantly, until the butter melts and the sauce thickens slightly, 2 to 3 minutes.

3. Pour the sauce over the cabbage and cook over medium heat, stirring constantly, until the cabbage wilts slightly and all the liquid has evaporated, 7 to 10 minutes. Taste, adding more vinegar or salt if you wish. Serve warm.

Cream Pie I

The Boston Cooking-School Cook Book, 1896

⅓ cup butter.

1 cup sugar.

2 eggs.

½ cup milk.

1¾ cups flour.

2½ teaspoons baking powder.

Mix as One Egg Cake. Bake in round layer cake pans. Put Cream Filling between layers and sprinkle top with powdered sugar.

ONE EGG CAKE

¼ cup of butter.

½ cup sugar.

1 egg.

½ cup of milk.

1½ cups flour.

2½ teaspoons baking powder.

Cream the butter, add sugar gradually, and egg well beaten. Mix and sift flour and baking powder, add alternately with milk to first mixture.

CREAM FILLING

⅞ cup sugar.

⅓ cup flour.

⅛ teaspoon salt.

2 eggs.

2 cups scalded milk.

1 teaspoon vanilla or ½ teaspoon lemon extract.

Mix dry ingredients, add eggs slightly beaten, and pour on gradually scalded milk. Cook fifteen minutes in a double boiler, stirring constantly until thickened, afterwards occasionally. Cool slightly and flavor.

THE ORIGINAL BOSTON CREAM PIE

This recipe is typical of Fannie Farmer's many cake recipes, which are simple by our standards but surprisingly satisfying. The recipe is in three parts, a classic example of Fannie's slightly tiresome cross-referencing system, which incorporates recipes from three different pages to make up the completed cake. Her Boston cream pie is not a pie at all, but a layer cake. Originally, it was probably baked in pie pans, hence the name. Accurate though Miss Farmer was about spoon and cup measurements, it was not until later editions of *The Boston Cooking-School Cook Book* that she added details on baking temperatures and the size of baking pans. Boston cream pie is best eaten when freshly baked.

SERVES 8

For the cake

1¾ cups/225 g flour, more for the pans

2½ teaspoons baking powder

⅓ cup/75 g butter, more for the pans

1 cup/200 g sugar

2 eggs, beaten to mix

½ cup/125 ml milk

For the cream filling
2 cups/500 ml milk
1 cup minus 2 tablespoons/175 g sugar
⅓ cup/45 g flour
⅛ teaspoon salt
2 eggs, beaten to mix
1 teaspoon vanilla or lemon extract
Powdered sugar, for assembly
Two 8-inch/20 cm round cake pans

1. Heat the oven to 350°F/175°C and set a rack in the center. Butter the pans, then line the bottoms with rounds of parchment or wax paper and butter the paper. Sprinkle the pans with flour and shake to coat them evenly; discard the excess.

2. Make the cake: Sift the flour with the baking powder into a bowl. In another bowl, with an electric mixer, cream the butter, then gradually beat in the sugar. Continue beating until the mixture is soft and light, 2 to 3 minutes. Beat in the eggs, a little at a time and at full speed, then continue beating 1 to 2 minutes. Using a metal spoon, alternately fold the flour mixture and the milk into the batter, in two or three batches.

3. Divide the batter between the pans, pushing the mixture to the sides with a spatula. Bake until the cakes are browned and spring back when lightly pressed with a fingertip, 30 to 35 minutes. Turn the layers onto a rack to cool, inverting them so the tops face up.

4. Meanwhile, make the cream filling: In a medium saucepan, bring the milk to a boil and let cool to tepid. In a bowl, stir together the sugar, flour, and salt. Make a well in the center and add the eggs, along with about half the cooled milk. Whisk, gradually drawing in the flour to make a smooth, stiff batter. Stir in the remaining milk. Return this mixture to the saucepan and cook over medium heat, whisking constantly, until the cream thickens. Continue cooking until the flour is thoroughly cooked and the custard coats the back of a spoon, 1 to 2 minutes. Let the custard cool, stirring often to pre-

vent a skin forming, then stir in the vanilla; the custard will stiffen on cooling.

5. To assemble the cake, spread the less attractive of the two layers with the cool cream and set the prettier layer on top. Press gently so the cream shows at the sides. Sprinkle the cake lightly with powdered sugar. Transfer the cake to a platter and cut into wedges for serving.

Bread and Butter Pudding

The Boston Cooking-School Cook Book, 1896

1 small stale baker's loaf.
Butter.
3 eggs.
½ cup sugar.
¼ teaspoon salt.
1 quart milk.

Remove end crusts from bread, cut loaf in one-half inch slices, spread each slice generously with butter; arrange in buttered pudding-dish, buttered side down. Beat eggs slightly, add sugar, salt, and milk; strain, and pour over bread; let stand thirty minutes. Bake one hour in slow oven, covering the first half-hour of baking. The top of pudding should be well browned. Serve with Hard or Creamy Sauce. Three-fourths cup raisins, parboiled in boiling water to cover, and seeded, may be sprinkled between layers of bread.

BREAD PUDDING WITH RAISINS

Most countries have a favorite use for stale bread and this one comes originally from England. It is no accident that Fannie Farmer specifies a stale loaf, so if in doubt, leave the slices to dry out overnight. The crusts add color to the pudding, while the raisins provide just the right kick of flavor. Miss Farmer suggests serving Hard Sauce with the pudding, or a Creamy Sauce for which she offers several versions. If serving a classic hard sauce of butter beaten with sugar and a flavoring, it's best to cut down on the butter in the pudding!

SERVES 8

¾ cup/100 g raisins

Stale 1-pound/450 g loaf white bread, cut in thick slices

6 tablespoons/90 g butter, more for the dish

3 eggs

½ cup/100 g sugar

½ teaspoon salt

1 quart/1 liter milk

7 x 11-inch/18 x 28 cm deep baking dish

1. Pour enough boiling water over the raisins to cover them and leave to soak for 30 minutes.

2. Generously butter the baking dish so the pudding does not stick.

3. Discard the end crusts from the loaf of bread, then spread each slice with butter and cut into 4 triangles. Drain the raisins.

4. Arrange the bread triangles, buttered side down and overlapping, in the baking dish, layering them with the raisins on all but the top layer. Whisk the eggs in a bowl until frothy, then whisk in the sugar and salt, followed by the milk. Spoon this custard over the bread triangles so they are evenly moistened, then leave until the custard is fully absorbed, about 30 minutes.

5. Heat the oven to 350°F/175°C and set a rack in the center.

6. Bake the pudding until thoroughly browned and bubbling in the center, 1 to 1¼ hours. Serve warm but not scorching hot.

IRMA ROMBAUER

1877–1962

Irma Rombauer with her daughter, Marion Rombauer Becker,
at a book signing.

RECIPES

Chapter 8

IRMA ROMBAUER

The Joy of Cooking

*The timeless guide to classic American recipes,
expanding on its predecessors to cover
cooking from coast to coast.*

In the history of successful cookbook authors, Irma Rombauer was a new phenomenon. She chronicled, and her own life epitomized, the food scene of the American Midwest in the early 1930s. Until then, almost all America's bestselling cookbooks originated in the eastern states, from New England running down into the South. Though perhaps unaware of it at the time, Mrs. Rombauer was writing for an audience that stretched from coast to coast. Her cooking did not harken back to the colonial traditions that had originated in Europe, as did Fannie Farmer and Mrs. Rutledge, but reflected the multicultural roots of a fairly recent United States. Expanding into multiple editions, *The Joy of Cooking*, later just *Joy of Cooking*, became the ultimate, unchallenged authority on simple American home cooking. And so it remains, for myself and for so many cooks.

All the best cookbooks capture the personal voice of the author, and Irma Rombauer joins their ranks. Irma was a lively, amusing woman and her chapter on cocktails opens: "Most cocktails containing liquor are made today with gin and ingenuity. In brief, take an ample supply of the former and use your imagination." And in the kitchen: "The cucumber," she comments, "is banned from any tables as indigestible, or even poisonous. Digestion, alas! is an individual matter." Irma thrived in the limelight, and she enjoyed travel. Throughout the 1930s and early 1950s she was on the move in Europe and Mexico. In later years her table was always open to visiting musicians, come to conduct the renowned symphony orchestra of St. Louis, the Missouri city where she spent much of her life.

Irma von Starkloff was born on October 30, 1877, a child of the south side of St. Louis, where she grew up with close ties to family in Germany. In the late 1880s, the Von Starkloffs spent four years in Bremen, where Irma's father was American consul. Back at home in 1899, she married a young lawyer named Edgar Rombauer and they had two children, Marion born in 1903, with Edgar Jr. arriving four years later. Irma Rombauer led a nonstop life, constantly moving from one project to another. She enjoyed company, joining the cultural Wednesday Club, and also the Unitarian Women's Alliance. With her friend Bella Tausig, she founded the Children's Lunch Association, later taken over citywide by the Board of Education. She had little, if any, culinary involvement, though she did, one summer in Michigan, take cooking classes with a neighbor, Mrs. Ray Johnson. From here blossomed her talent for decorating cakes (cascades of wild roses were a favorite theme; Irma enjoyed plants and gardening).

Edgar Rombauer, sadly, did not share Irma's gregarious nature. He was subject to depression and in 1930 he committed suicide. The Wall Street crash of 1929 had depleted what funds the Rombauers possessed, and when Edgar was gone, Irma was left with about $6,000 to her name. Instead of looking for a job, she decided to assemble a cookbook. When she was first married, Irma had had no idea how to cook, but her husband, who had experience with cooking over an open fire on camping trips, lent a hand. After more than thirty years of marriage, Irma had amassed a pile of recipes that she had collated for the Women's Alliance in St. Louis.

Irma needed space to reflect, so she retreated far from friends and family to an obscure inn in Michigan. She had five hundred recipes at her disposal, and she opted for drafting them in the style made familiar by Fannie Farmer, in which the ingredients are listed under the title with the active instructions in running text below. Fannie had been the pioneer of this style, and Irma cemented it as the almost universal pattern for cooks of the future, though some later editions of *The Joy of Cooking* were to waver from this simplicity. From time to time Irma adds a short opening note to her recipes to set the scene: "This is a good way of utilizing leftover sweet potatoes. Serve them to people who like pumpkin, for they are not unlike pumpkin pie filling." By no means do all subjects earn such detailed treatment, so that Roast Turkey or Rabbit Stew consist of useful notes rather than precise recipes. The great strength of *The Joy of Cooking* is that the simple, down-to-earth instructions are utterly reliable. What is more, the coverage is far-reaching—this is the place to track down traditional favorites.

So valued were homemade cakes in middle-class kitchens that *The Joy of Cooking*'s general instructions on Sponge Cakes run to almost two pages before the reader even reaches a recipe. The advice is meticulous and exhaustive, designed to reassure the debutante cook. "Do not beat a sponge cake batter until the recipe calls for it." "Have a cake pan ready." "Add the sugar slowly and beat or work it into the butter until it is entirely dissolved. This first step in the making of a butter cake is very important—do not hasten it," Mrs. Rombauer cautions severely.

The authorship of *The Joy of Cooking* is a story of not just one woman, but two. Irma's daughter, Marion Rombauer Becker, was involved with the book from the first draft of 1930. She tested recipes while studying art in New York. On return to St. Louis the following winter, she created the black-and-white illustrations, a dancing procession of courtiers and chefs, rabbits and swimming fish in silhouette, that give the chapter headers such impact. Hers was the Art Deco cover design for the first edition, in which the blue-robed St. Martha of Bethany, the patron saint of cooks and domestic servants, is seen slaying the brilliant green dragon of kitchen drudgery. Now you know whom to evoke in moments of kitchen despair!

"How naive and straightforward was our approach to publishing!" exclaims Marion Rombauer Becker. When she and her mother had their manuscript in order, they called an unknown printer and signed a contract for three thousand copies. The book might have languished in quiet obscurity if Irma Rombauer had not, one day, been playing bridge with the president of the Bobbs-Merrill publishing group. The modest privately printed edition of 1931 became transformed by 1936 into the behemoth that we know today. In Irma's self-effacing words, "So the record, which to begin with was a collection such as every kitchen-minded woman possesses, has grown in breadth and bulk until it now covers a wide range."

After their first successful cookbook, most authors embark on a second, focusing on a different theme. Not so Irma Rombauer. She knew what her audience valued and she was determined to deliver it to them by adding more and more of her tried-and-true recipes. The first trade edition of 1936 had run to 640 pages and sold more than 50,000 copies. A 1943 edition contained about 3,350 recipes at 884 pages and featured wartime rationing tips. Over the years both Irma and Marion worked on more revisions, adjusting recipes to changing times. Finally, with the 1951 edition, Irma announced, "I'm finished." Like many women cookbook authors, Irma Rombauer published her cookbook relatively late in life and she knew when to stop. She had been fifty-four when the first edition of *The Joy of Cooking* appeared in 1931. Little did she realize how far-reaching and long-lived her influence would be.

She took advantage of retirement to enjoy a last grand tour of Europe with her fifteen-year-old grandson, Ethan Becker, who was to become closely involved with the future development of later editions. In Paris, long before the appearance of *Mastering the Art of French Cooking*, they met a fellow American named Julia Child over lunch with her soon-to-be coauthor Louisette Bertholle. (What they ate was not recorded, but perhaps it might have been Dover sole meunière, the dish that so enchanted Julia on her first visit to France.) Meanwhile, edition followed edition with Marion Rombauer Becker gradually taking over. She had been acknowledged as coauthor as early as the third revision in 1951 and *The Joy of Cooking* continued to sell well.

Bobbs-Merrill, the longtime publisher of *The Joy of Cooking*, had been having management troubles since the early 1950s, and in 1962 new leadership took over. Marion Rombauer Becker had some radical changes in mind. She had devised a clever index card system to present the recipes to the publisher, but no one at Bobbs-Merrill seemed qualified to assess it, nor to approve it as a substitute for a full-blown manuscript. This was a complication, but worse, the greatly expanded length of the manuscript would incur higher costs to publish. It was just at this moment in 1962 that Irma Rombauer died. Bobbs-Merrill heedlessly rushed a new edition to press, before Marion had had time to check and approve the revised proofs. The standoff can only be imagined. It took a great deal of discussion and exercise of good will for a revised edition to appear in 1963 incorporating Marion's changes. Sales reached well over 100,000 copies, and continued rising to 145,630 in 1964, with increases each year until the next edition in 1974.

No cookbook in American history had achieved such fame. Two decades later *Joy of Cooking* was chosen by the New York Public Library during their centennial celebration in 1995 as the only cookbook among its 150 most influential books of the century. More than a million copies had been sold by the time the seventh edition was published in 1997. After a series of revisions, a 75th anniversary edition was published in 2006. It contained 1,152 pages and more nearly echoed earlier editions. The urge to modernize was curbed and the teaching text was restored and expanded. As Julia Child put it when she heard about the upcoming anniversary edition: "Thanks for putting the joy back in JOY."

Many revisions of the original *The Joy of Cooking* have come and gone, with sections such as Know Your Ingredients, and Brunch, Lunch, and Supper making appearances from time to time. The freezer, the pressure cooker, and the food processor now play roles, while the contribution of frozen and canned foods are accepted. Meals in thirty minutes or less are emphasized. Tastes have changed, not to mention dietary trends. In Mrs. Rombauer's day, the primary concern was to create economical, nourishing meals that were appealing to the family, but she also offered recipes for entertaining. Lobster Newburg runs side by side on the page with Codfish Balls and "Shrimp Wiggle." More diverse ethnic dishes have entered the American repertoire as well as the pages of *Joy of Cooking*, with recipes such as risotto Milanese, taramasalata, petits fours, and even a Becker gyro sandwich. The family continues to be involved, with Ethan Becker listed as coauthor with his grandmother Irma Rombauer and mother, Marion Rombauer Becker, on the 2006 edition. Irma's great-grandson John Becker and his wife, Megan, spearheaded a new edition in 2019. Total sales of all editions are estimated by the current publisher Scribner to be 18 million copies.

And so continues the life story of *The Joy of Cooking*, with the core vision retained. In 1997, an attempt at modernizing the concept was made, but readers were adamant; they valued the original, the simple home cooking with recipes that are easy to execute and appealing to family tastes. No matter what edition we consult (early editions fetch a tidy sum on eBay), the recipes are easy to execute and appeal to family tastes. Foolproof recipes for Baked Macaroni, Hollandaise Sauce, Swiss Steak, and Chocolate Cake (the Rombauer family favorite) can be crucial for busy home cooks. Julia Child always said that *The Joy of Cooking* was her first cookbook. It was, she maintained: "A fundamental resource for any American cook," and so it remains. The original full title ran *The Joy of Cooking: A Compilation of Reliable Recipes with a Casual Culinary Chat*. "Will it encourage you," asked Irma Rombauer in one of her prefaces, "to know that I was once as ignorant, helpless and awkward a bride as was ever foisted on an impecunious lawyer?" That tells it all. Encouraged, aspiring cooks continue to "stand facing the stove," as her first instruction reads.

Cream of Tomato Soup without Soda

The Joy of Cooking, 1931

2 cups of tomatoes
2 teaspoons sugar
½ onion (medium sized)
2 large ribs of celery with leaves

Boil these ingredients for 15 minutes. Meanwhile prepare:

4 tablespoons flour
4 tablespoons butter
4 cups milk or milk and cream scalded
1 teaspoon salt
⅛ teaspoon paprika

Melt the butter in the top of a double boiler over a low fire, add the flour and when these ingredients are well blended add the scalded milk. Stir this until it is thick and smooth. When the tomato mixture is ready, strain it into the milk mixture. Add the seasoning and place the top part of the double boiler on the bottom part, which has been filled with boiling water. Cover the soup with a lid and serve it in fifteen minutes.

NOTE: Recipes for Tomato soup usually call for soda (¼ teaspoon). I have experimented carefully and have made good soup without it by the above method, thereby retaining the delicate flavor of the soup.

TOMATO SOUP

Irma Rombauer's recipe raises all sorts of modern-day questions, and is a clear example of different days, different ways. What, for example, did the "double boiler" look like that was large enough to hold 2 cups of tomatoes and a quart of milk? Presumably, it was a roasting pan of hot water with a saucepan set inside, or what we would call a water bath.

Irma decries the use of baking soda, commonly added in the old days to balance the acidity of unripe tomatoes. Today we rely on ripe fruit. She seasons with just ⅛ teaspoon of paprika, which would surely get you nowhere. My adaptation takes into account today's quicker methods and more vivid seasonings and the resulting soup is unexpectedly delicious—when did you last taste a fresh tomato soup?

SERVES 6 TO 8

4 to 6 large ripe tomatoes (about 2 pounds/900 g), cored and chopped (including skins and seeds)
2 stalks celery with leaves attached, chopped
½ onion, chopped
2 teaspoons sugar
Salt
1 quart/1 liter milk
4 tablespoons/60 g butter
¼ cup/30 g flour
½ teaspoon paprika, or more to taste

1. In a large saucepan, stir together the chopped tomatoes, celery, onion, sugar, and a little salt. If the tomatoes are not very juicy, add ½ cup/125 ml water. Cover and simmer the mixture, stirring often, until the vegetables are very soft, 20 to 30 minutes, depending on the ripeness of the tomatoes.

2. Meanwhile, in a saucepan, scald the milk. In a separate saucepan, melt the butter, then whisk in the flour and cook over medium heat until bubbling, 1 to 2 minutes. Whisk in the warm milk and bring

to a boil, whisking constantly, until the sauce thickens. Add 1 teaspoon salt and the paprika and simmer the white sauce gently so the flour is thoroughly cooked, 1 to 2 minutes.

3. In a food processor, purée the tomato mixture and work it through a coarse sieve into a bowl. Stir the purée into the white sauce, taste and adjust the seasoning. The soup is delicious when freshly made. If reheated, it may curdle, but the texture can be restored with a handheld blender.

Beef Loaf II

The Joy of Cooking, 1931

4 TO 6 SERVINGS

1 pound beef ground (¼ of this may be pork)
3 carrots
1 stalk dwarf celery
2 small potatoes
½ onion
1 tablespoon chopped parsley
Salt, paprika

Put the vegetables through a food chopper, combine them with the remaining ingredients and shape them into a loaf. Bake the loaf for one hour in a moderate oven 350°. Baste the loaf frequently with stock, or tomato juice. Make the gravy with the drippings—Page 154.

GRAVY

Strain the stock into a saucepan and place the pan in cold water. This will cause the fat to rise. Skim it carefully and use it as a basis for the gravy in about the following proportions:

3 tablespoons fat
2 tablespoons flour
1 cup strained stock
Seasoning

Heat the fat, add the flour and when this bubbles, add the stock. Stir the gravy until it is thick and smooth. When making gravy from fat meats, it will sometimes separate. This looks calamitous, but it is easily remedied. Add a little cream very slowly, stirring all the time, and the gravy will become smooth and thick. Taste the gravy and if it is not good, make it so. Add paprika, celery salt, catsup, (sparingly) beef cubes, or Savita, give it character. Having made it good, a great deal has been accomplished, but not enough, it must also look good. Keep a bottle of Kitchen Bouquet on hand. Add enough of this to make the gravy a fine color and it is ready to serve. Never over-season or add unnecessarily to good gravy. Doctor only the indifferent ones and color them to make them attractive. If you have no Kitchen Bouquet, a little burnt sugar will serve the purpose. There is no excuse, except inefficiency, for a whitish, lumpy, tasteless gravy, but one encounters them, alas, in endless varieties. Therefore these instructions.

MEATLOAF

Meatloaf is a blank slate for the home cook: I like to follow Mrs. Rombauer in suggesting some pork mixed with beef for richness, and plenty of celery for taste and crunch. Chopping the vegetables in a food processor is even easier than the tabletop grinders of the 1930s. Serve meatloaf hot with mashed potatoes and gravy, or at room temperature in a sandwich.

SERVES 6

Oil for the baking pan
¾ pound/330 g ground beef
¼ pound/110 g ground pork
3 carrots
2 small potatoes
1 small stalk celery
½ medium onion
1 tablespoon chopped parsley
2½ teaspoons salt
2 teaspoons paprika
1 cup/250 ml tomato juice or beef stock,
    or more if needed for basting

For the gravy
3 tablespoons drippings from the pan
2 tablespoons flour
1 cup/250 ml beef stock
Cream (optional)
Paprika (optional)
Celery salt (optional)
Medium baking pan

1. Heat the oven to 350°F/175°C and set a rack in the center. Oil the baking pan.

2. Put the ground beef and pork in a large bowl.

3. Cut the carrots, potatoes, celery, and onion in chunks and mix them together in a bowl. Using a food processor, cut the vegetables to a medium chop in two or three batches. Dip your hands in cold water and stir the chopped vegetables into the beef and pork. Sprinkle with the parsley, salt, and paprika and mix again.

4. Arrange the beef mixture lengthwise in the baking pan, shaping it with wet hands into a loaf about 3 inches/7.5 cm high and 5 inches/13 cm wide. Pour over the tomato juice or stock. Bake, basting from time to time, until the loaf is browned and starting to shrink, 1 to 1¼ hours. A metal skewer inserted in the center should be warm to the touch when withdrawn.

5. If serving hot, transfer the meatloaf to a platter and cover with foil to keep warm. Alternatively, let the meatloaf cool and serve it at room temperature.

6. Make the gravy: Measure 3 tablespoons of drippings into the pan, set over medium heat, stir in the flour and when this bubbles, stir in the stock. Continue stirring until the gravy is thick and smooth, 3 to 5 minutes. If the gravy separates, slowly stir in a little cream. Season with paprika or celery salt, if you like. Serve the meatloaf on a platter with the gravy in a separate bowl.

Bread Rolls—(Never fail)

The Joy of Cooking, 1931

18 SMALL ROLLS

These rolls, incredibly light in texture, are not unlike a brioche. They require no kneading:

I. Dissolve 1 cake yeast in ¼ cup lukewarm water
II. Dissolve
¼ cup lard
1¼ teaspoon salt
2 tablespoons sugar, by pouring 1 cup boiling water over
   them

When II is lukewarm, combine it with I. Use a wire whisk to beat in 1 egg and about 2¾ cups flour, (enough flour to make a soft dough). Place the dough in a large bowl, cover it with a plate and set it in the icebox—(the dough will treble in bulk). Chill it from 2 to 12 hours. Pinch off small pieces of dough with buttered hands and place them in greased muffin tins, filling the tins about one-third full. Cover the tops with melted butter and permit the rolls to rise for about 2 hours. Bake them in a hot oven 450° until they are crisp and brown.

NEVER-FAIL DINNER ROLLS

The idea of a yeast bread roll that never fails is hard to resist (later editions use shortening instead of lard). And so is a dough that is mixed without kneading, leading to puffy rolls with an enviable crumb. The best bet is to let the rolls rise slowly in a warm corner of the kitchen (around 65°F/18°C) and bake them at the last minute so they come to the table warm from the oven. The rolls will puff up while baking and will look like muffins.

MAKES 18 ROLLS

For the yeast
1 tablespoon/10 g active dry yeast
½ cup/125 ml tepid water

For the dough
1 cup/250 ml water
¼ cup/60 g lard
2 tablespoons sugar
1¼ teaspoons salt
3 cups/375 g flour, or more if needed
1 egg, beaten to mix
1½ sticks/¾ cup/170 g melted butter, for muffin tins,
    your hands, and for brushing rolls
18 medium muffin cups

1. Dissolve the yeast: Sprinkle the yeast over the tepid water in a small bowl and leave about 5 minutes.

2. Make the dough: In a small saucepan, heat the water, lard, sugar, and salt until the lard is melted. Let cool to tepid, then stir in the dissolved yeast.

3. Put the flour in a large bowl (the dough will later double in bulk) and make a well in the center. Add the yeast mixture and the egg and mix with your hand, gradually drawing in the flour to make a smooth dough. It should be soft but not sticky, so work in more flour if needed. Cover with plastic wrap and leave in a warm place to rise until doubled in bulk, 1 to 2 hours. If preparing ahead, transfer the dough to the refrigerator and store up to 12 hours.

4. To shape the rolls, butter the muffin cups and your hands. Pinch off small pieces of dough, roll in balls, and drop them in the muffin cups, filling each cup one-third full. Brush the tops with melted but-

ter and leave the rolls to rise in a warm place until doubled in bulk, 30 to 45 minutes.

5. Heat the oven to 450°F/240°C and set a rack in the center.

6. Bake the rolls until browned and pulling from the sides of the cups, 12 to 15 minutes. Let the rolls cool a few moments, then unmold them. Serve while still warm if possible.

Corn Flake Drops

The Joy of Cooking, 1931

3 egg whites
1½ cups sugar
4 cups corn flakes, rolled (measured before rolling)
1 cup nut meats or 1 cup shredded cocoanut
1 teaspoon vanilla

Beat the egg whites until stiff, add the sugar very slowly, and then fold in the remaining ingredients. Drop the batter from a teaspoon onto greased baking sheets. Bake the cakes in a slow oven 325°.

CORN FLAKE COOKIES

Where would we be without corn flakes? Invented in the late eighteen hundreds, as a healthy breakfast option for vegetarians at the Battle Creek Sanitarium in Michigan, corn flakes were one of America's first convenience foods. For the nuts, either pecans or walnuts do well as an alternative to coconut in this recipe.

MAKES ABOUT 30 COOKIES

Butter for the baking sheet
4 cups/140 g corn flakes
3 egg whites
1½ cups/300 g sugar
1 teaspoon vanilla
1 cup/100 g shredded coconut or 1 cup/150 g pecan or walnut pieces

1. Heat the oven to 325°F/160°C and set a rack low down. Line a baking sheet with parchment paper and butter the paper.

2. Put the corn flakes in a plastic bag and pound with a rolling pin until coarsely crushed.

3. In a bowl, whisk the egg whites just until stiff. While whisking, gradually pour in the sugar to make a soft, shiny meringue, about 30 seconds. Stir in the vanilla, then fold in the coconut or nut pieces, followed by the crushed corn flakes.

4. Drop heaping tablespoons of the mixture onto the prepared baking sheet. Bake until dry and slightly puffed, 15 to 16 minutes; they should not brown and should be slightly soft in the center when cool. Let the cookies cool on the baking sheet for 2 to 3 minutes, then transfer them to a rack to cool completely. The cookies will keep several days in an airtight container.

Delmonico Ice Cream

The Joy of Cooking, 1931

6 TO 7 SERVINGS

2 egg yolks

4 tablespoons cream

3½ tablespoons powdered sugar

1 teaspoon vanilla, or 1 tablespoon Sherry

1 cup cream, whipped

2 egg whites, whipped

Beat the egg yolks with the sugar, add the 4 tablespoons of cream and beat this mixture well. Place it in a double boiler and cook it until it is smooth and slightly thickened, stirring it constantly. Remove it from the fire and cool it. Add the vanilla and chill it. Whip the cream and the egg whites in separate bowls until they are very stiff. Combine them lightly and fold in the custard.

ICE CREAM BOMBE

The custard base in this recipe does not need to be stirred in a churn during freezing, so in culinary terms, the dessert would be called a bombe rather than an ice cream. Vanilla extract is a familiar flavoring, but sherry is a subtle twist. This is a fancy recipe for special occasions and a nice accompaniment to berries or a classic pound cake.

SERVES 6 TO 8

4 eggs, separated

6 tablespoons/75 g powdered sugar

2½ cups/625 ml heavy cream

4 teaspoons vanilla extract or ¼ cup/60 ml sherry

1. In a metal or heatproof glass bowl, whisk the egg yolks and powdered sugar until thick and light, about 1 minute. Beat in ½ cup/125 ml of the cream. Set the bowl over a pan of simmering water and heat the mixture, stirring, until it thickens to coat the back of a wooden spoon, 2 to 3 minutes. Remove from the heat and let the mixture cool. Chill a serving bowl.

2. Whip the remaining cream until it holds a soft peak. Whisk the egg whites until just stiff, then fold into the cream. Fold this mixture into the cooled egg yolk mixture along with the vanilla or sherry. Transfer it to the chilled serving bowl, cover tightly, and freeze. The bombe will keep up to 3 days in the freezer. Serve chilled.

JULIA CHILD

1912–2004

Julia was always happy in the kitchen.

RECIPES

Potage Velouté aux Champignons, page 185

Ratatouille, page 189

Coq Au Vin, page 193

Thon à la Provençale, page 198

La Tarte des Demoiselles Tatin, page 203

Cream of Mushroom Soup, page 187

Ratatouille, page 191

Coq au Vin, page 196

Tuna Provençale, page 200

Caramelized Upside-Down Apple Tart, page 207

Chapter 9

JULIA CHILD

Mastering the Art of French Cooking

The definitive guide that established French cooking principles at home and rekindled America's love of good food.

Julia Child led two lives. The first was as a sociable international house-wife. The second began when, at the age of fifty-one, she appeared on a public television show and became a celebrity. At six feet two inches tall with an inimitable warbling voice, Julia was immediately recogniz-able wherever she went. She was born on August 15, 1912, in Pasadena, California. Raised as a patrician Republican, Julia spent three years of World War II in the Office of Strategic Services and toured Europe with her diplomat husband, Paul. While abroad, she discovered the delights of French cuisine and the challenge of transferring them to print. Endowed with legendary natural talent, she only had to appear on screen once to become an instant star.

Julia Carolyn McWilliams was the oldest child of three, with a brother, John, two years younger and a beloved sister, Dorothy (known as Dort). After graduating from Smith College in 1934, Julia worked part time in advertising in New York and toyed with the idea of becom-ing a novelist when World War II intervened. Julia was too tall for mili-tary service so she volunteered for the OSS (forerunner of the CIA) and was sent to Ceylon (now Sri Lanka) and then on to China. It was there she met Paul Child, her ideal partner in and out of the kitchen.

Paul was four inches shorter and ten years older than she was, but had many attributes that Julia admired. He was well traveled, sophisticated, amusing, and enjoyed good food. On returning to the United States, they remained friends, visiting Julia's father and stepmother (Julia's own mother, Caro, had died when Julia was in her midtwenties). Paul and Julia's relationship deepened and in 1945 they announced their intention to marry. "About time!" was the family's reaction. After his postwar move into the US Foreign Service, Paul was sent to Paris in 1948 as part of the US Information Service.

Paul was Julia's passport to French cooking. Fresh off the boat in France, their first meal was a classic: oysters on the half shell, *sole meunière*, local cheeses, and a *tarte aux pommes*. When Paul explained (he was fluent in French) that the lengthy conversation overheard at the next table was about the choice of wine, Julia exclaimed: "Wine! At lunch!" Once installed in their little Parisian apartment on the rue de l'Université, Julia became restless. Museums were all very well, but she longed for activity. She and Paul would have welcomed children but it was not to be. "At least I had time for a career," she declared. She enrolled at Le Cordon Bleu in the six-week professional course—it was cheaper than the one for tourists. Her instructor was Chef Max Bugnard who had been trained by Escoffier. Her culinary education continued at home, thanks to Paul's gourmet commentary on the food she set on his plate.

Through the embassy social circuit, Julia met two Frenchwomen who were working on a cookbook and looking for an American collaborator. Simone Beck (Simca) became a lifelong friend, a gold mine of knowledge on French cuisine. The other woman, Louisette Bertholle, was talkative but inclined to be absent when there was hard work to be done. And work there was when the trio created a sprightly cooking school for American ladies, "L'École des Trois Gourmandes," at a fee of $5 per class. Julia and Simca took turns teaching in Simca's apartment with original recipes such as Poulet à la Bouillabaisse and Artichauts Braisés à la Provençale.

Julia also took charge of helping craft a book on French cooking for Americans that Simca and Louisette had started but couldn't quite master. It began to take shape, with Julia developing an original recipe style in which the ingredients and equipment were singled out in boldface type on the left-hand side of the page, and method instructions on the right. A generous opening paragraph put the dish in context, suggesting accompaniments and hints about the seasons. Julia had a clear vision of what she wanted: "This is a book for the servantless American cook who can be unconcerned on occasion with budgets, waistlines, time schedules, children's meals, the parent-chauffeur-den-mother syndrome or anything else which might interfere with the enjoyment of producing something wonderful to eat."

Julia and Simca tested, retested, revised, and recast their text, taking seven years before the 850-page manuscript was ready. Over time, Louisette was less and less involved. Julia envisioned multiple volumes and had to be restrained. Even so, such a book was a major investment for a publisher and an offer proved hard to find. Julia was an avid letter writer and one of her longtime correspondents in Boston, Avis DeVoto, had arranged an introduction to Houghton Mifflin. But the manuscript was too unwieldy to convince the food editor there. After more revisions, a young editor named Judith Jones at Alfred A. Knopf in New York became interested, leading to a lifelong partnership. After much debate about a title for the book, it was Judith who suggested *Mastering the Art of French Cooking*. In 1961, Paul retired and he and Julia settled in a generous clapboard house in Cambridge, Massachusetts, where they entertained many friends and distinguished intellectuals, including economist John Kenneth Galbraith and historian Arthur Schlesinger. A few years later in 1966, down in Washington, DC, I was newly married and the editor of the *Washington Star* and part of this social scene.

Chez Julia-in-Cambridge, meals were a happy blend of recently tested recipes such as Quiche Lorraine, Boeuf Bourguignon, and the chocolate cake Reine de Saba, mixed in with the freshest Massachusetts fish and meat from her nearby artisan butcher, Mr. Savenor ("honeymoon roast" of trimmings from beef filet was one of his specialties). Visitors were made welcome, offered a drink appropriate to the hour, and then put to work, be it peeling vegetables, stirring a simmering pot, or simply sitting to talk so everyone was kept happy. Paul's domain was the butler's pantry, where he would create the house specialty, a "reverse martini" of iced dry vermouth with a whiff of gin and twist of lemon. Physically tireless, Julia would be the first person downstairs at breakfast, firing up the large black teapot on the back of her stove. I quite often stayed the night at Julia's and can attest that she was the last to go to bed and always the first to put the kettle on in the morning.

A year after publication, *Mastering the Art* had been doing respectably. It was named a Book of the Month Club Selection in 1962 and twelve thousand copies had been distributed (though not necessarily sold). On February 11, 1962, Julia was invited by Professor Albert Duhamel to appear on his evening TV show *I've Been Reading* on WGBH, a public television station in Boston. Julia agreed but insisted she would not just talk but must also cook. When told there were no facilities, she insisted: "We'll do an omelet in an electric skillet." After that episode, twenty-seven viewers wrote to the station wanting to see more. The station produced three pilot episodes with the catchy title *The French Chef*, shooting them in the Boston Gas Company's kitchen. Julia was a natural.

The show debuted locally in 1962 and then went national in 1963. Julia always disliked the title: "I'm not a chef!" she said, but she was stuck with it. Teaming up with Russ Morash as director and Ruth Lockwood as producer, *The French Chef* ran for more than ten years and two hundred shows. Episodes can still be downloaded on iTunes. Early on, the phrase "Bon Appétit!" became Julia's signature sign off. Budget restrictions were tight and equipment was at a minimum. When filming, Paul would crawl between the set and the camera sending signals on what he and Julia called Idiot Cards (cue cards) with instructions such as "Wrong saucepan" and "30 seconds left" as the camera ran for twenty-six minutes exactly, no stopping and no reshoots. Julia's gifts of improvisation were invaluable. There was the memorable moment she dropped a loaded platter. "Never mind," she said scooping it off the floor and looking at the camera: "No one is here but you and me."

At Thanksgiving 1966, Julia's portrait, painted by Boris Chaliapin, appeared on the cover of *Time* magazine. Knopf ordered another printing of forty thousand copies of *Mastering the Art* instead of the usual ten thousand. French cooking was sweeping America. In the White House, the Kennedys had installed René Verdon, a French chef. This was the beginning of a wave of enthusiasm for ethnic styles of cooking across the nation. France was followed many years later by the freshness and simplicity of Italy, summed up in print by Marcella Hazan, next it was Chinese and other Asian cuisines. Cooking schools proliferated, adult education programs offered classes, and supermarkets devoted aisles to newly popularized ingredients such as lemongrass and fresh ginger. Today the Internet abounds with educational opportunities, from simple techniques like chopping an onion to weeks of full-scale online classes with diplomas at the end. But the concept of cooking in your own kitchen following instructions on a screen goes back to Julia Child.

In the mid-1960s, Paul and Julia's love affair with France continued. After a couple of years, *Mastering the Art* had accumulated some serious royalties, so Julia and Paul decided to invest in a modest place in Provence, leasing land on the property near Grasse where Simca lived. La Pitchoune ("The Little Thing" in Provençal) was just that, a simple three-bedroom cottage, shaded by old trees with a terrace view. The kitchen, with its solid square cast-iron stove, was at the back, away from the heat of the sun. "La Peetch" as Julia and Paul called it, was the perfect escape from the increasing demands of book writing and television appearances in the United States. When Paul developed heart trouble and gradually slowed down, Julia, too, adjusted her way of life. She rarely left his side and whenever traveling, she would call him daily until he died in Boston in 1994.

In light of Julia's success, by the mid-1960s Judith Jones was begging for a new book. So in 1967 *The French Chef Cookbook* was born, a compilation of recipes from the television series. More important, Julia was working on *Mastering the Art of French Cooking, Volume Two* and complaining that with her insistence on perfection it would never be ready for the publication date of 1970. In parallel, a new version of *The French Chef* was launched, this time in color. In 1978 the series was named *Julia Child & Company* and featured menu ideas for occasions varying from Dinner for the Boss, to a Cocktail Party, and a Buffet for the curious number of 19. With her usual thoroughness, Julia also covered subjects such as leftovers and definitive instructions on how to poach an egg. All these series were accompanied by cookbooks featuring the recipes. Then in 1989, a more personal book of Julia's appeared: *The Way to Cook* covered new ideas, products, and equipment (gadgets always intrigued Julia; she loved the Cuisinart).

Working with Julia on any project, on or off television, could be a challenge. She herself was enormously organized, with everything ready in the background, even down to breaking for lunch, sitting at a properly set table with a glass of red wine for all (she issued written instructions in advance). She was a perfectionist. When she came to teach with me at La Varenne resort at the Greenbrier in West Virginia, a serving dish was needed for Choufleur Polonaise, a reassembled boiled cauliflower topped with melted butter, chopped hard-boiled egg, and parsley. When an oval serving dish was offered, she recoiled, "No!" she objected, "we need a round dish, a cauliflower is round." My abiding memory is of my crawling on the floor trying to locate the right platter in the closet. As prepared as Julia always was, she also valued spontaneity. Needless to say she loved a grand display, and some of hers were unforgettable. When the subject of a class was variety meats, she had the whole twenty-foot countertop covered with ice on which to display not just the usual sweetbreads and kidneys, but all four of the cow's stomachs, the ears, cheek, whole oxtail, heart, lungs, liver, udder, and more unmentionables. One day when roasting chicken in an electric oven at full throttle, she flung open the door and cast a cupful of cold water into the bottom to form steam to crispen the chicken skin. All her helpers, and her large audience, put their heads down awaiting the explosion from a short circuit, but Julia was born lucky—all was well.

In 1982, Julia had begun a monthly column for *Parade* magazine, a task she particularly enjoyed because it reached kitchens throughout America. When meeting fans Julia was outgoing and talkative, exactly as on the screen, but she was instinctively private—if anyone asked her a personal question (and many did), she would turn her reply into a question for the interlocutor. Quite late in life, when she was eighty-eight, Julia was given the French Légion d'Honneur, the highest French national medal. She was also awarded the American Medal of Freedom during George W. Bush's presidency. Julia, a devoted Democrat, was skeptical, but after he called she reported, "Why," she said, "he was very nice!"

In that same year, Julia partnered with her longtime friend Chef Jacques Pépin in *Jacques & Julia Cooking at Home*, with an amiable take on soufflés, Châteaubriand steak, and other classics of the French repertoire.

Julia's energy had always seemed boundless and she scarcely slowed until, in 2001, she entered a retirement home in Santa Barbara, California, that she and Paul had booked into years before. The Santa Barbara climate resembled Provence, and so did the mimosa to Julia's delight. Julia died on August 14, 2004, one day shy of her ninety-second birthday. Her last meal was a bowl of homemade French onion soup, a simple dish of half a dozen ingredients that is a true test of a good cook.

Julia's reputation saw another renaissance after her death with the 2009 movie *Julie & Julia*, inspired by a blog written by a young New Yorker, Julie Powell. Realizing she knew almost nothing about cooking, Julie decided to work her way through all 524 recipes of *Mastering the Art*, taking 365 days and recording the experience on her blog. Julia might have enjoyed *Julie & Julia*, seeing Meryl Streep's brilliant performance as the towering, throaty Julia in an Academy Award–nominated role. *Mastering the Art* had never hit the *New York Times* bestseller list in Julia's lifetime, but the book rocketed to the top almost forty-eight years after it was originally published.

The parallel portrayed so successfully in *Julie & Julia* was no accident. Here was the master cook revealing her secrets. It neatly summed up Julia's career, her deep, instinctive understanding of French cuisine with its relish for every aspect of good food. Julia's gift to the cooks that followed her was her uncanny grasp of the essentials of a dish, allied with her ability to communicate them on paper and so vividly on the screen. She loved to instance a baguette loaf, as explained from time to time to French school children. First you look at it: Is it evenly golden brown, not too dark, but not pale? Is it evenly risen, with five (not four nor six) even slashes for rising? Then you sniff its heady, yeasty aroma. Next you pinch it to be sure it is crispy but yielding, not dry or flabby.

Then you pull apart a piece to test elasticity, and finally you taste. The new season's flour is quite different from the old, the salt, the yeast, even the water can make a difference. It was this degree of detail, these subtle distinctions that Julia was such an expert at unraveling for the novice cook.

"I don't believe in anything beyond," she had declared a few days before she died. "It's life that matters."

JULIA'S KITCHEN

Julia's husband, Paul, designed their kitchen in Cambridge, Massachusetts. Meals were taken around a scrubbed wooden table covered with oilcloth; a giant Garland professional range occupied one side with the sink on the other and a window above. On one wall was Julia's signature pegboard, designed by Paul, pierced with hooks and marked with the outline of the pots to be hung from them. At one end of the table was the modern oven at eye level so the soufflé or roast chicken could be observed from moment to moment. When Julia left Cambridge in 2001 for retirement in the California sun, her iconic kitchen was added to the Smithsonian's National Museum of American History in Washington DC, where visitors flock to share and reflect on all that Julia inspired.

Potage Velouté aux Champignons
[Cream of Mushroom Soup]

Mastering the Art of French Cooking, Volume One, 1961

Here is a fine, rich, mushroom soup, either for grand occasions or as the main course for a Sunday supper.

FOR 6 TO 8 PEOPLE

A 2½-quart, heavy-bottomed enameled saucepan
¼ cup minced onions
3 Tb butter

Cook the onions slowly in the butter for 8 to 10 minutes, until they are tender but not browned.

3 Tb flour

Add the flour and stir over moderate heat for 3 minutes without browning.

6 cups boiling white stock or chicken stock; or canned chicken
     broth and 2 parsley sprigs, ⅓ bay leaf, and ⅛ tsp thyme
Salt and pepper to taste
The chopped stems from ¾ to 1 lb. fresh mushrooms

Off heat, beat in the boiling stock or broth and blend it thoroughly with the flour. Season to taste. Stir in the mushroom stems, and simmer partially covered for 20 minutes or more, skimming occasionally. Strain, pressing juices out of mushroom stems. Return the soup to the pan.

2 Tb butter
An enameled saucepan
The thinly sliced caps from ¾ to 1 lb. fresh mushrooms
¼ tsp salt
1 tsp lemon juice

Melt the butter in a separate saucepan. When it is foaming, toss in the mushrooms, salt, and lemon juice.

Cover and cook slowly for 5 minutes.

Pour the mushrooms and their cooking juices into the strained soup base. Simmer for 10 minutes.

(*) If not to be served immediately, set aside uncovered, and film surface with a spoonful of cream or milk. Reheat to a simmer just before proceeding to the step below, which will take 2 or 3 minutes.

2 egg yolks
½ to ¾ cup whipping cream
A 3-quart mixing bowl
A wire whip
A wooden spoon

Beat the egg yolks and cream in the mixing bowl. Then beat in hot soup by spoonfuls until a cup has been added. Gradually stir in the rest. Correct seasoning. Return the soup to the pan and stir over moderate heat for a minute or two to poach the egg yolks, but do not let the soup come near the simmer.

1 to 3 Tb softened butter
Optional: 6 to 8 fluted mushroom caps, page 510, cooked in
     butter and lemon juice; and/or 2 or 3 Tb minced fresh
     chervil or parsley

Off heat, stir in the butter by tablespoons. Pour the soup into a tureen or soup cups, and decorate with optional mushroom and herbs.

CREAM OF MUSHROOM SOUP

When *Mastering the Art of French Cooking* was launched in 1961, button mushrooms were a gourmet item in the grocery store. The equivalent today would be an exotic mushroom such as fresh chanterelles or even porcini—either would be a treat to replace the button mushrooms in this soup. A liaison is a binder, and here Julia uses a classic combination of egg yolks and cream to add richness to the pungent mushrooms just before the soup is served. Do not try reheating this liaison, as it will curdle.

MAKES NEARLY 2 QUARTS/2 LITERS SOUP
  TO SERVE 6 TO 8

1 pound/450 g mushrooms
⅓ cup/75 g butter
1 medium onion, finely chopped
3 tablespoons flour
1½ quarts/1.5 liters chicken stock
Salt and pepper
Juice of ½ lemon

For the liaison
2 egg yolks
¾ cup/175 ml heavy cream

2 tablespoons chopped parsley or chervil, for serving

1. Trim the mushroom stems level with the caps and chop the stems.
2. In a large saucepan, melt half the butter. Add the chopped onion and sauté until soft but not brown, 2 to 3 minutes. Whisk in the

flour and cook, stirring, until frothy, about 1 minute. Stir in the stock, bring the soup to a boil, and stir in the mushroom stems. Half cover the pan, reduce the heat, and simmer about 20 minutes.

3. While the stock is simmering, slice the mushroom caps. In a skillet, melt the remaining butter and add the sliced mushrooms with a little salt, pepper, and a squeeze of lemon juice. Cover and cook over low heat, stirring once or twice, until the juice runs from the mushrooms and they are wilted, 8 to 10 minutes.

4. Strain the soup into a bowl, pressing hard to extract all the liquid. Discard the solids. Pour the liquid back into the pan and add the cooked sliced mushrooms with their liquid. Taste, adjust the seasoning with salt, pepper, and lemon juice, and simmer 10 minutes. Taste again. The soup can be prepared 2 days ahead to this point and refrigerated, or it can be frozen.

5. Just before serving, make the liaison: Bring the soup back to a boil. In a small bowl, whisk the egg yolks and cream and stir in 3 to 4 tablespoons of the hot soup. Off the heat, whisk this liaison back into the rest of the soup; it will both thicken and enrich the soup. Do not boil the soup again, as it will curdle. Spoon the soup into bowls and sprinkle with parsley for serving.

Ratatouille
[Eggplant Casserole—with tomatoes, onions, peppers, and zucchini]

Mastering the Art of French Cooking, Volume One, 1961

Ratatouille perfumes the kitchen with the essence of Provence and is certainly one of the great Mediterranean dishes. As it is strongly flavored it is best when it accompanies plain roast or broiled beef or lamb, *pot-au-feu* (boiled beef), or plain roast, broiled, or sautéed chicken.

Equally good hot or cold, it also makes a fine accompaniment to cold meats, or may be served as a cold hors d'oeuvre.

A really good *ratatouille* is not one of the quicker dishes to make, as each element is cooked separately before it is arranged in the casserole to partake of a brief communal simmer. This recipe is the only one we know of which produces a *ratatouille* in which each vegetable retains its own shape and character. Happily a *ratatouille* may be cooked completely the day before it is to be served, and it seems to gain in flavor when reheated.

FOR 6 TO 8 PEOPLE

½ lb. eggplant
½ lb. zucchini
A 3-quart, porcelain or stainless steel mixing bowl
1 tsp salt

Peel the eggplant and cut into lengthwise slices ⅜ inch thick, about 3 inches long, and 1 inch wide. Scrub the zucchini, slice off the two ends, and cut the zucchini into slices about the same size as the eggplant slices. Place the vegetables in a bowl and toss with the salt. Let stand for 30 minutes. Drain. Dry each slice in a towel.

A 10- to 12-inch enameled skillet
4 Tb olive oil, more if needed

One layer at a time, sauté the eggplant, and then the zucchini in hot olive oil for about a minute on each side to brown very lightly. Remove to a side dish.

½ lb. (about 1½ cups) thinly sliced yellow onions
2 (about 1 cup) sliced green bell peppers
2 to 3 Tb olive oil, if necessary
2 cloves mashed garlic
Salt and pepper to taste

In the same skillet, cook the onions and peppers slowly in olive oil for about 10 minutes, or until tender but not browned. Stir in the garlic and season to taste.

1 lb. firm, ripe, red tomatoes, peeled, seeded, and juiced,
    page 505 (makes 1½ cups pulp)
    Salt and pepper

Slice the tomato pulp into ⅜-inch strips. Lay them over the onions and peppers. Season with salt and pepper. Cover the skillet and cook over low heat for 5 minutes, or until tomatoes have begun to render their juice. Uncover, baste the tomatoes with the juices, raise heat and boil for several minutes, until juice has almost entirely evaporated.

A 2½ quart fireproof casserole about 2½ inches deep
3 Tb minced parsley

Place a third of the tomato mixture in the bottom of the casserole and sprinkle over it 1 tablespoon of parsley. Arrange half of the eggplant and zucchini on top, then half the remaining tomatoes and parsley. Put in the rest of the eggplant and zucchini, and finish with the remaining tomatoes and parsley.

Salt and pepper

Cover the casserole and simmer over low heat for 10 minutes. Uncover, tip casserole and baste with the rendered juices. Correct seasoning, if necessary. Raise heat slightly, and cook uncovered for about 15 minutes more, leaving a spoonful or two of flavored olive oil. Be careful of your heat; do not let the vegetables scorch in the bottom of the casserole.

(*) Set aside uncovered. Reheat slowly at serving time, or serve cold.

RATATOUILLE

In the introduction, Julia Child sums up the essence of ratatouille and we can imagine her surrounded by vegetables from the market, sautéing them one by one in a colorful enameled cast-iron casserole. The ratatouille can be kept in the casserole for serving warm or at room temperature.

SERVES 6 TO 8

1 medium eggplant (about 1 pound/450 g)
3 to 4 small zucchini (about 1½ pounds/675 g)
1 teaspoon salt
½ cup/125 ml olive oil, more if needed
3 green bell peppers (about 1 pound/450 g), cored and sliced
1 medium onion (about ½ pound/225 g), sliced
3 to 4 cloves garlic, chopped
Salt and pepper
2 to 3 large, very ripe tomatoes (about 1½ pounds/675 g)
2 to 3 tablespoons chopped parsley
Medium enameled cast-iron casserole or Dutch oven

1. Trim and peel the eggplant with a vegetable peeler. Cut it lengthwise into ⅜-inch/8 mm slices, about 3 inches/7.5 cm long and 1 inch/2.5 cm wide. Rinse and trim the zucchini, then cut them into slices about the same size as the eggplant. Put the eggplant and zucchini in a bowl, toss with the salt, and leave them 30 minutes—salt draws out the juices. Drain the eggplant and zucchini and dry them on paper towels.

2. In a large skillet, heat 2 or 3 tablespoons of the oil. Add the eggplant and zucchini and sauté over brisk heat, browning them lightly and adding more oil as needed, 1 to 2 minutes on each side. Set the eggplant and zucchini aside.

3. Add the peppers and onions to the skillet with a little more oil and sauté, stirring often, until tender and the onions are starting to brown, 8 to 10 minutes. Stir in the garlic and season with salt and pepper.

4. Peel, seed, and coarsley chop the tomatoes. Spread them on top of the peppers and onions and cook over low heat until the tomato juices start to run, about 5 minutes. Increase the heat and cook, stirring, until most of the juice has evaporated, 3 to 5 minutes. Set the tomato mixture in a bowl.

5. Oil the casserole and spread one-third of the tomato mixture in the bottom. Sprinkle some parsley on the tomato mixture, then top with half the eggplant and zucchini. Add half the remaining tomato mixture, sprinkle with parsley, and top with the remaining eggplant and zucchini. Make a final layer with the remaining tomato mixture and sprinkle with parsley. Cover the casserole and simmer over low heat for 10 minutes.

6. Uncover and baste the vegetables with their juices. Taste and adjust the seasonings. Continue simmering, uncovered, until the vegetables are moist and tender, about 15 minutes longer—if overcooked, the vegetables will become soggy. Serve the ratatouille, very warm or at room temperature, in the casserole. It will keep up to 2 days in the refrigerator; warm it slightly before serving as chilling may subdue the flavor.

Coq Au Vin
[Chicken in Red Wine with Onions, Mushrooms, and Bacon]

Mastering the Art of French Cooking, Volume One, 1961

This popular dish may be called *coq au Chambertin, coq au ries-ling,* or *coq au* whatever wine you use for its cooking. It is made with either white or red wine, but the red is more characteristic. In France, it is usually accompanied only by parsley potatoes; buttered green peas could be included if you wish a green vegetable. Serve with it a young, full-bodied red Burgundy, Beaujolais, or Côtes du Rhône.

FOR 4 TO 6 PEOPLE

A 3- to 4-ounce chunk of lean bacon

Remove the rind and cut the bacon into *lardons* (rectangles ¼ inch across and 1 inch long). Simmer for 10 minutes in 2 quarts of water. Rinse in cold water. Dry.

A heavy, 10-inch, fireproof casserole or an electric skillet
2 Tb butter

Sauté the bacon slowly in hot butter until it is very lightly browned (temperature of 260 degrees for an electric skillet). Remove to a side dish.

2½ to 3 lbs. cut-up frying chicken

Dry the chicken thoroughly. Brown it in the hot fat in the casserole (360 degrees for the electric skillet).

½ tsp salt
⅛ tsp pepper

Season the chicken. Return the bacon to the casserole with the chicken. Cover and cook slowly (300 degrees) for 10 minutes, turning the chicken once.

¼ cup cognac

Uncover, and pour in the cognac. Averting your face, ignite the cognac with a lighted match. Shake the casserole back and forth for several seconds until the flames subside.

3 cups young, full-bodied red wine such as Burgundy,
   Beaujolais, Côtes du Rhône, or Chianti
   1 to 2 cups brown chicken stock, brown stock, or canned
      beef bouillon
   ½ Tb tomato paste
   2 cloves mashed garlic
   ¼ tsp thyme
   1 bay leaf

Pour the wine into the casserole. Add just enough stock or bouillon to cover the chicken. Stir in the tomato paste, garlic, and herbs. Bring to the simmer. Cover and simmer slowly for 25 to 30 minutes, or until the chicken is tender and its juices run a clear yellow when the meat is pricked with a fork. Remove the chicken to a side dish.

12 to 24 brown-braised onions, page 483
   ½ lb. sautéed mushrooms, page 513

While the chicken is cooking, prepare the onions and mushrooms.

Salt and pepper

Simmer the chicken cooking liquid in the casserole for a minute or two, skimming off fat. Then raise heat and boil rapidly, reducing the liquid to about 2¼ cups. Correct seasoning. Remove from heat, and discard bay leaf.

3 Tb flour
2 Tb softened butter
A saucer
A rubber spatula
A wire whip

Blend the butter and flour together into a smooth paste (*beurre manié*). Beat the paste into the hot liquid with a wire whip. Bring it to the simmer, stirring, and simmer for a minute or two. The sauce should be thick enough to coat a spoon lightly.

Arrange the chicken in the casserole, place the mushrooms and onions around it, and baste with the sauce.

(*) If the dish is not to be served immediately, film the top of the sauce with stock or dot with small pieces of butter. Set aside uncovered. It can now wait indefinitely.

Shortly before serving, bring to the simmer, basting the chicken with the sauce. Cover and simmer slowly for 4 to 5 minutes, until the chicken is hot through.

Sprigs of fresh parsley

Serve from the casserole, or arrange on a hot platter. Decorate with sprigs of parsley.

COQ AU VIN

Every French cook has their own version of Coq au Vin and, as you would expect, Julia includes the full garnish of baby onions, bacon, and mushrooms. Perhaps she would have used a bottle of the robust Provençal red wine made near her French home, La Pitchoune. Julia simmers the chicken on top of the stove, but I suggest cooking the chicken in the oven, as it requires less attention. In the introduction to her recipe, Julia herself defines the best accompaniments for the sumptuous sauce—parsleyed potatoes and a full-bodied red wine.

SERVES 4 TO 6

3- to 4-pound/1.35 to 1.8 kg roasting chicken, cut into 6 to 8 pieces
Salt and pepper
4 very thick slices bacon, cut in strips (lardons)
1 tablespoon vegetable oil
15 to 18 baby onions (about 375 g), peeled
½ pound/225 g button mushrooms, quartered
¼ cup/60 ml Cognac
1 (750 ml) bottle full-bodied red wine
2 to 3 cloves garlic, chopped
1 teaspoon tomato paste
1½ to 2 cups/375 to 500 ml chicken stock, or more if needed
Bouquet garni of 2 to 3 parsley stems, 4 to 6 sprigs thyme, and 1 bay leaf, tied with string

For the kneaded butter
3 tablespoons butter, at room temperature
3 tablespoons flour
1 to 2 tablespoons chopped parsley, for garnish
Medium oval or round flameproof casserole

1. Sprinkle the chicken pieces with salt and pepper.
2. Place the bacon strips in a small saucepan of cold water. Bring to a

boil and simmer for 8 to 10 minutes to remove salt and soften the bacon. Drain and dry on paper towels.

3. In the casserole, heat the oil over medium heat. Add the onions and bacon and brown them, 6 to 8 minutes. Remove the onions and bacon from the casserole and set aside. Add the mushrooms to the casserole and fry until wilted and their juices have evaporated, 5 to 7 minutes. Add the mushrooms to the onions and bacon.

4. Heat the oven to 325°F/160°C.

5. Working in batches if needed, put the chicken pieces in the casserole over medium-high heat and brown them thoroughly on all sides, 12 to 15 minutes. Pour over the Cognac, standing back in case it flames. Add the wine and boil until reduced by half, 8 to 10 minutes. Add the garlic, then stir in the tomato paste, followed by the stock. Tuck the bouquet garni down beside the chicken. Bring to a simmer, then cover the pot and transfer to the oven and bake, turning the chicken once or twice, until the meat is very tender, 1 to 1¼ hours. The meat will be pulling from the leg bones, and the chicken juices will run clear when you prick the legs with a two-pronged fork. If some pieces are tender before others, remove them and set aside while the rest continues to cook. If the casserole gets dry, add more stock.

6. Transfer the chicken pieces to a tray and cover with foil to keep warm. Discard the bouquet garni. Skim off any fat from the top of the cooking liquid.

7. Make the kneaded butter: With a fork, knead the butter, then work in the flour to make a paste. With the casserole over medium heat, whisk pieces of the paste into the simmering stock for at least 5 minutes until it is thick enough to coat the back of a wooden spoon.

8. Drain the onions, bacon, and mushrooms, then stir them into the sauce. Taste the sauce and adjust the seasoning. Put the chicken pieces back into the casserole and heat gently until the chicken is very hot, 4 to 5 minutes. Serve from the casserole, or in a deep serving dish, sprinkled with chopped parsley.

Thon à la Provençale
[Tuna or Swordfish Steaks with Wine, Tomatoes, and Herbs]

Mastering the Art of French Cooking, Volume One, 1961

Tomatoes, wine, herbs, and garlic are a good contrast to tuna or swordfish, and this dish can be served either hot or cold. Boiled potatoes and green beans would go well, and a chilled *rosé* wine, or a dry white such as *côtes de Provence*, or Riesling.

FOR 6 TO 8 PEOPLE

3 lbs. fresh tuna or swordfish cut into steaks ¾ inch thick (if fish is
    frozen, thaw it)
A 9- by 14-inch pyrex baking dish about 2½ inches deep
1 tsp salt
2 Tb lemon juice
6 Tbs olive oil
⅛ tsp pepper

Remove skin, and cut fish steaks into serving pieces. Blend salt and lemon juice in baking dish, then beat in the oil and pepper. Arrange the fish in the dish, and baste with the marinade. Cover with waxed paper and marinate 1½ to 2 hours, turning and basting the fish with the marinade several times. Drain the fish and dry it thoroughly on paper towels. Discard the marinade, which will be strong and fishy.

3 to 4 Tb olive oil, more if needed
A skillet

Sauté the fish rapidly in very hot olive oil for a minute or two on each side to brown lightly. Rearrange the fish in the baking dish.

Preheat the oven to 350 degrees.

1 cup minced yellow onions
3 lbs. fresh, ripe red tomatoes peeled, seeded, juiced, and
    chopped, page 505
2 cloves mashed garlic
½ tsp oregano
¼ tsp thyme
¼ tsp salt
⅛ tsp pepper

Cook the onions slowly in the skillet for 5 minutes or so until tender but not browned. Stir in the tomato pulp, garlic, seasonings, and herbs. Cover skillet and cook slowly for 5 minutes. Correct seasoning, and spread the tomato mixture over the fish.

1 cup dry white wine or ⅔ cup dry white vermouth

Place a cover or aluminum foil over the baking dish and bring to the simmer on top of the stove. Then set in lower third of preheated oven and bake for 15 minutes. Pour in the wine and bake for 30 minutes more, turning oven down to 325 degrees as soon as fish is simmering.

A serving platter

Remove fish to a serving platter, scraping the sauce off the fish and back into the baking dish. Keep fish warm for about 5 minutes while finishing the sauce.

1 to 2 Tb tomato paste for added flavor and color
Optional: 1 Tb meat glaze, page 110, for depth of flavor

Boil down the sauce over high heat until it has reduced to about 2 cups. Stir in the tomato paste and optional meat glaze. Simmer for a moment, and correct seasoning.

1 Tb flour blended to a paste with 1 Tb softened butter
2 to 3 Tb chopped parsley

Off heat, beat in the flour and butter paste, and bring again to the simmer for 1 minute. Stir in the chopped parsley, spoon the sauce over the fish, and serve.

(*) Fish may be set aside, then covered and reheated in the oven, but be careful not to overcook it.

Other Fish—green cod or coalfish, ocean pollack, and halibut may be cooked in the same way. They need no marinating and require only 20 to 30 minutes of baking.

TUNA PROVENÇALE

The days of giant fresh tuna steaks, such as those suggested by Julia, are sadly long gone, but this simple recipe suits smaller ones, too, or indeed any thickly cut steak of swordfish, shark, or halibut. When cut under ½ inch thick, any fish tends to dry out too fast in the oven, so I recommend thicker pieces. Marinating the fish for an hour or two before baking also helps keep it moist. Julia discards the marinade as "fishy," but I like to continue using it, as I'm parsimonious in the kitchen. I bake the fish for a far shorter time, because today we're used to lightly done tuna.

SERVES 3 TO 4

Grated zest and juice of ½ lemon
¼ cup/60 ml olive oil
Salt and pepper
3 or 4 tuna steaks cut ¾ inch/2 cm thick (about 1½ pounds/675g
    total)

For the tomato topping
1 tablespoon olive oil
1 small onion, chopped
1 clove garlic, chopped

3 large tomatoes (about 1½ pounds/675 g), peeled, seeded, and
   chopped
½ tablespoon chopped fresh oregano
½ tablespoon chopped fresh thyme
Salt and pepper

For assembly
1 tablespoon olive oil
½ cup/125 ml robust white wine, such as Chardonnay

For the sauce
1 tablespoon tomato paste
Salt and pepper
½ tablespoon flour
½ tablespoon butter
2 tablespoons chopped parsley

1. In a small bowl, whisk together the lemon zest, lemon juice, and
   olive oil and season with salt and pepper. Lay the tuna steaks in
   a dish, pour over the marinade, and turn the steaks to coat them
   on both sides. Cover and refrigerate, turning once or twice, 1 to 2
   hours.

2. Heat the oven to 350°F/175°C and set a rack in the center.

3. Make the tomato topping: In an ovenproof medium skillet, heat
   the olive oil. Add the onion and fry, stirring often, until starting to
   brown, 5 to 7 minutes. Stir in the garlic and cook until fragrant,
   about 1 minute. Stir in the tomatoes, oregano, and thyme, and season with salt and pepper. Cook until the tomatoes soften, 5 to 7
   minutes. Remove from the heat, taste, and adjust the seasoning.
   Transfer the tomato mixture to a bowl and set aside.

4. To assemble, first brown the tuna steaks: Wipe out the skillet and
   heat the olive oil until almost smoking. Without discarding the marinade, lay the tuna steaks in the skillet and brown 1 to 2 minutes.
   Turn and brown the other side, about 1 minute. Stop cooking, then

pour the reserved marinade over the fish and spread the tomato mixture on top, followed by the white wine. Transfer to the oven and bake until the tuna steaks are done to your taste, rare or fully cooked, 10 to 15 minutes. To test, flake the fish with a fork.

5. Place the tuna steaks on a serving platter, leaving the tomato mixture and juices in the skillet, and cover the fish with foil to keep warm.

6. Make the sauce: Reduce the tomato mixture in the skillet down to about 1 cup/250 ml, then stir in the tomato paste and season to taste with salt and pepper. Simmer for 1 minute, then remove from the heat. Blend the flour and butter to a paste, then whisk this paste into the tomato mixture and stir in the parsley. Season to taste with salt and pepper.

7. To serve, mound a spoonful of tomato mixture on the fish while still warm.

La Tarte des Demoiselles Tatin
[Upside-down Apple Tart—hot or cold]

Mastering the Art of French Cooking, Volume One, 1961

This is an especially good tart if your apples are full of flavor. It is cooked in a baking dish with the pastry on top of the apples. When done, it is reversed onto a serving dish and presents a lovely mass of caramelized apples.

FOR 8 PEOPLE

4 lbs. crisp cooking or eating apples
⅓ cup granulated sugar
Optional: 1 tsp cinnamon

Quarter, core, and peel the apples. Cut into lengthwise slices ⅛ inch thick. Toss in a bowl with the sugar and optional cinnamon. You should have about 10 cups of apples.

2 Tb softened butter
A baking dish 9 to 10 inches in diameter and 2 to 2½
    inches deep (pyrex is practical, as you can see when the
    tart is done)
½ cup granulated sugar
6 Tb melted butter

Butter the baking dish heavily, especially on the bottom. Sprinkle half the sugar in the bottom of the dish and arrange a third of the apples over it. Sprinkle with a third of the melted butter. Repeat with a layer of half the remaining apples and butter, then a final layer of the apples and butter. Sprinkle the rest of the sugar over the apples.

Preheat oven to 375 degrees.

Chilled sweet short paste (proportions for 1 cup of flour),
page 633

Roll out the pastry to a thickness of ⅛ inch. Cut it into a circle the size of the top of the baking dish. Place it over the apples, allowing its edges to fall against the inside edge of the dish. Cut 4 or 5 holes about ⅛ inch long in the top of the pastry to allow cooking steam to escape.

Aluminum foil, if needed

Bake in lower third of preheated oven for 45 to 60 minutes. If pastry begins to brown too much, cover lightly with aluminum foil. Tart is done when you tilt the dish and see that a thick brown syrup rather than a light liquid exudes from the apples between the crust and the edge of the dish.

A fireproof serving dish
Powdered sugar, if needed

Immediately unmold the tart onto serving dish. If the apples are not a light caramel brown, which is often the case, sprinkle rather heavily with powdered sugar and run under a moderately hot broiler for several minutes to caramelize the surface lightly.

2 cups heavy cream, or *crème fraîche*, page 16

Keep warm until serving time, and accompany with a bowl of cream. (May also be served cold, but we prefer it warm.)

PÂTE BRISÉE SUCRÉE
[Sweet Short Paste]

Sweet short paste is made exactly like the regular short paste except that sugar is mixed into the flour before you begin.

Amounts Needed
For an 8- to 9-inch shell, proportions for 1½ cups flour
For a 10- to 11-inch shell, proportions for 2 cups flour

Proportions for 1 cup flour
1 cup (3½ ounces) sifted all-purpose flour
A mixing bowl
1 Tb granulated sugar
⅛ tsp salt
5½ Tb fat; 4 Tb chilled butter and 1½ Tb chilled
    vegetable shortening
2½ to 3 Tb cold water

Place the flour in the bowl, mix in the sugar and salt, then proceed to make the dough and mold the shell as described and illustrated on pages 140–145.

From page 140–145:

Directions for making short paste
The mixing of pastry should be accomplished rapidly, particularly if your kitchen is warm, so that the butter will soften as little as possible. Use very quick, light finger movements, and do not linger on the dough at all with the warm palms of your hands. A pastry blender may be used if you wish, but a necessary part of learning how to cook is to get the feel of the dough in your fingers. *Il faut mettre la main à la pâte!*

Place the flour, salt, sugar, butter, and vegetable shortening in a big mixing bowl. Rub the flour and fat together rapidly between the tips of your fingers until the fat is broken into pieces the size of oatmeal flakes. Do not overdo this step as the fat will be blended more thoroughly later.

Add the water and blend quickly with one hand, fingers held together and slightly cupped, as you rapidly gather the dough into a mass. Sprinkle up to 1 tablespoon more water by droplets over any unmassed remains and add them to the main body of the dough. Then press the dough firmly into a roughly shaped ball. It should just hold together and be pliable, but not be damp and sticky.

Place the dough on a lightly floured pastry board. With the heel of one hand, not the palm which is too warm, rapidly press the pastry by two-spoonful bits down on the board and away from you in a firm, quick smear of about 6 inches. This constitutes the final blending of fat and flour, or *fraisage*.

With a scraper or spatula, gather the dough again into a mass; knead it briefly into a fairly smooth round ball. Sprinkle it lightly with flour and wrap it in waxed paper. Either place it in the freezer compartment of the refrigerator for about 1 hour until the dough is firm but not congealed, or leave it for 2 hours or overnight in the refrigerator.

Uncooked pastry dough will keep for 3 to 4 days under refrigeration, or may be frozen for several weeks. In either case, wrap it airtight in waxed paper and a plastic bag.

Rolling out the dough

Because of its high butter content, roll out the dough as quickly as possible, so that it will not soften and become difficult to handle.

Place the dough on a lightly floured board or marble. If the dough is hard, beat it with the rolling pin to soften it. Then knead it briefly into a fairly flat circle. It should be just malleable enough so that it can be rolled out without cracking.

Lightly flour the top of the dough. Place the rolling pin across center and roll the pin back and forth with firm but gentle pressure to start the dough moving. Then, with a firm, even stroke, and always rolling away from you, start just below the center of the dough and roll to within an inch of the far edge.

Lift dough and turn it at a slight angle.

Give it another roll. Continue lifting, turning, and rolling, and as necessary, sprinkle board and top of dough lightly with the flour to prevent sticking. Roll it into a circle ⅛ inch thick and about 2 inches larger all around than your pie pan or flan ring. If your circle is uneven, cut off a too-large portion, moisten the edge of the too-small portion with water, press the two pieces of pastry together, and smooth them with your rolling pin.

The dough should be used as soon as it has been rolled out, so that it will not soften.

CARAMELIZED UPSIDE-DOWN APPLE TART

There are two keys to a great Tarte Tatin. One is to use an apple variety that remains firm during cooking, while the other is to thoroughly brown the caramel so the sugar loses much of its sweetness—this happens during baking. For firm apples, I recommend Granny Smith, Melrose, Winesap, or Braeburn. A pie pan at least 2 inches/5 cm deep is needed and a heatproof glass version works well. This recipe is quite complicated but amply rewards the effort.

SERVES 8

For the sweet pie pastry
1 cup/125 g flour, more for rolling
1 tablespoon sugar
½ teaspoon salt
4 tablespoons/60 g chilled butter, diced small, more for the pan
1½ tablespoons chilled shortening, cut in small dice
2 tablespoons cold water, or more if needed

For the tart
10 small apples (about 3½ pounds/1.6 kg)
1 teaspoon ground cinnamon (optional)
¾ cup/150 g sugar
⅓ cup/75 g butter, melted, more for the pan
1 cup/250 ml crème fraîche, for serving
9-inch/23 cm pie pan at least 2 inches/5 cm deep

1. Make the sweet pie pastry: Put the flour in a bowl and sprinkle over the sugar and salt. Add the butter and shortening and toss to mix. Continue tossing with your fingertips to make crumbs, pulling them apart until as fine as oatmeal flakes. Sprinkle over the water and continue mixing until the dough holds together in a ball, adding a little more water if needed. The dough should be soft but not sticky.

2. Turn the dough onto a floured work surface and knead it lightly, pushing it away with the heel of your hand, gathering it up and giving it a half turn. Repeat this action 4 or 5 times until the fat has been mixed into the flour. Shape the dough into a ball, wrap it in a kitchen towel, and refrigerate until firm, 15 to 20 minutes.

3. Form the tart: Peel, quarter, and core the apples, then cut them lengthwise in ⅛-inch/3 mm slices. Put the slices in a bowl and toss with the cinnamon (if using) and half the sugar. Generously butter the pie pan and sprinkle with the remaining sugar. Arrange one-third of the apples in concentric circles in the pan like the petals of a flower and drizzle with one-third of the melted butter. Add half the remaining apple slices, spreading them in an even layer, and drizzle with half the remaining butter. Add the rest of the apples, with all of their juices, then drizzle with the remaining butter. Press the apples so they're in a flat even layer and set the pan aside.

4. Sprinkle a work surface with flour and roll the pastry dough to a 10-inch/25 cm round. Lift the dough onto the pie pan, on top of the apples, making sure the edges fall inside the rim of the dish. With scissors, snip 4 or 5 holes near the center to allow steam to escape. Refrigerate the tart 15 to 20 minutes.

5. Heat the oven to 425°F/220°C and set a rack quite low down.

6. Bake the tart until the pastry is browned and you can see when you lift the crust that a thick brown caramel is leaking from the apples, 1 to 1¼ hours. If the pastry gets very brown during baking, cover it loosely with foil.

7. Let the tart cool 5 to 10 minutes. Set a deep platter on top of the pan and carefully invert it so the caramelized apples are on top and the pastry is on the bottom. Serve the tart warm, or at room temperature, with the crème fraîche on the side.

EDNA LEWIS

1916–2006

The kitchen was home to Edna Lewis.

RECIPES

Chapter 10

EDNA LEWIS

The Taste of Country Cooking

*The work that expanded the scope of regional cookbooks
to include personal style as an essential element
of writing about good food.*

Right from the start of *The Taste of Country Cooking* Edna Lewis brings her personal voice into the kitchen. She talks of a modest feast: "There was always a cool evening brought on by a heavy thunderstorm and this would be a night for a boiled ham. The meat with the skin on was often served warm and invariably thought to taste more delicious with new boiled vegetables and the first peach cobbler of the summer." It is with irresistible stories like this that Edna Lewis was to win fame, influencing the style of so many cookbook writers of the future.

The background of Southerner Edna Lewis, granddaughter of slaves, is a far cry from the secure middle- and upper-class backgrounds of women cookbook writers before her. She was born in 1916 in the settlement of Freetown, Virginia, the land that had been granted by a nearby plantation owner to a group of newly freed slaves just after the Emancipation of 1863. Nearly sixty years later, little had changed. "Ours was a large family," writes Edna in the introduction of *The Taste of Country Cooking*, "my parents, my grandfather, three sisters, two brothers, and cousins who stayed with us from time to time, all living under the same roof. The farm was demanding but everyone shared in the work—

tending the animals, gardening, harvesting, preserving the harvest, and, every day, preparing delicious food that seemed to celebrate the good things of each season." They lived on ingredients that could be raised or grown in the backyard, chickens, and turkeys that nested in the woods (it was Edna and the other children's job to ensure the birds' survival). And the family raised pigs: Lard was the foundation fat, extracted from the generous layer that lined the animal's skin. It was heated very slowly, leaving delicious crispy morsels of crackling to nibble. One of Edna's favorites was Crackling Bread and woe betide the cook who scorched the lard. For the young Edna, cooking was inseparable from the earth and the seasons: First came the wild asparagus, the leafy tops of baby beets, then new potatoes, wild strawberries, fillets of shad, that rare and succulent fish that runs in the spring. Early summer would bring let-tuces, cucumbers, the first corn and tomatoes, followed by stone fruits, the peaches and plums that mark the start of the preserving season. My own childhood was spent in similar rural seclusion, half a mile from the nearest farmhouse in Yorkshire, during World War II. But living off the land in northern England was far less abundant than the American South. My mother grew peas and runner beans, with onions in the rose bed. Pears and apples ripened only one year in two as late frost nipped the blossoms. She would shoot at early-rising rabbits from her bedroom window, but rarely bagged a hit. Looking back, it was a prime example of living off whatever the land could offer, as did Edna's family.

In Edna's balmy home state of Virginia, every farmstead had an arbor of vines, the grapes growing loose on the stems so they could be picked as they ripened, little by little. In *The Taste of Country Cooking* she lists the old varieties, red, golden, and black, with their expected dates of ripening. The crisp, juicy flesh of watermelon was a particular treat, as was hand-churned ice cream (the ice had to be carted in from the nearby town of Lahore, then chipped into chunks to layer with salt in the bucket around the ice cream churn). By autumn and the begin-ning of hunting season, the walnuts and pecans were ready, in time for the celebration meals of Harvest Festival and finally Christmas, bring-ing dishes such as Roast Capon, Plum Pudding, and Nut Butter Balls. Edna is focused on the kitchen; she scarcely mentions the wet and dry

years, the bugs, the seeds that do not germinate as hoped. But like anyone who lives off the land, she must have been instinctively aware of
the weather.

Edna Lewis's parents, Chester and Lucinda Lewis, were illiterate,
but they had opened part of their home to Isabella Lightfoot, a black
graduate of Oberlin College, for use as a school for their family and the
community children. After Chester Lewis died in 1928, Lucinda and
the six surviving children must have struggled, particularly when the
Depression hit in the early '30s. At age sixteen, Edna Lewis joined what
became known as the Great Migration north—several family members
worked in Washington DC, so that was her first stop. Before long Edna
was in New York City, and became part of the social scene thanks to
her dressmaking talents, and later her skill in the kitchen. Along the
way, she became involved with politics and the extreme left. During
the 1930s she married Steve Kingston, a retired merchant seaman and
a Communist.

From the beginning, little Edna had loved to cook, and she had
picked up the considerable skills of her mother and her Aunt Jenny by
helping in the kitchen in Freetown. In New York, Edna's dinner parties were renowned, and among the regular guests was Johnny Nicholson who in 1948 was planning to open a café on the Upper East Side.
He installed Edna at the stove of the newly opened Café Nicholson
and soon she was serving her herbed roast chicken, filet mignon, and
a legendary chocolate soufflé like the one her mother used to make.
(The French touch was chic in New York at the time. In Virginia it
had lingered as a legacy from the colonial era when the elite socialized
with French politicians before the Revolutionary War.) Thus began a
star-studded career for Edna Lewis—once Gore Vidal even asked her if
she had studied in Paris. Celebrities ranging from Marlene Dietrich to
Tennessee Williams, Greta Garbo, Howard Hughes, Truman Capote,
Salvador Dalì, and even Eleanor Roosevelt flocked to Café Nicholson.

Edna's cooking was instinctive, a matter of sight and smell and
touch, and of course experience. At home there had been no measuring
spoons, baking powder had been measured on a coin. In 1972 her first
cookbook appeared, entitled *The Edna Lewis Cookbook* and coauthored

by Evangeline Peterson, a former student from the cooking classes Edna gave from time to time in New York. The book was a modest collection of around one hundred recipes, showcasing Southern favorites such as Oysters on the Half Shell Broiled with Buttered Breadcrumbs, Roast Ribs of Pork with Peanut Sauce, and Deep-Dish Apple Pie with Nutmeg Sauce. The pages revealed that Edna was a natural storyteller. "Fried chicken was considered a special dish in Virginia," she remarks, "because until the 1920s frying chickens—like lamb—were available only in the late spring and early summer; hence the term "spring chicken." And the reader can picture young Edna, out in the early summer dawn: "An essential ingredient to tasty corn on the cob is its freshness. Ideally, corn should be picked just before cooking, but when this is not possible, try to buy corn that has been picked at dawn and then refrigerated."

Unassuming as *The Edna Lewis Cookbook* might be, it was much praised by luminaries such as James Beard, and it led Edna to Judith Jones, the senior editor at Alfred A. Knopf, who was the doyenne of cookbook editing. Her authors included Julia Child, Claudia Roden, Madhur Jaffrey, Lidia Bastianich, and Marcella Hazan, as well as (in translation) Jean-Paul Sartre and Albert Camus. Edna was by now renowned, a noted personality with upswept dark hair tinged with gray and a brilliant smile. She was all the more impressive for her penchant for flowing dresses in bright colors that emphasized her height, and even Judith Jones was "a little awed by her."

When Judith and Edna met, it was Judith who detected the treasury of knowledge behind Edna's formidable appearance, and it was she who coaxed Edna to write down not just her recipes, but the stories behind them. The resulting manuscript, originally handwritten on yellow legal pads, became *The Taste of Country Cooking*, a timeless record of Southern cooking that has remained the classic authority for nearly fifty years. "I sensed immediately from her pleasure in these memories that Edna must be a wonderful cook," wrote Judith in her preface to *Country Cooking*, an evocation of Ms. Lewis's childhood in the 1920s, a world that had almost disappeared by the time the book was published in 1976. Edna Lewis closes her introduction saying, "I hope this book will be helpful . . . but above all, I want to share with everyone who may read this a time and a place that is so very dear to my heart." Her dedication is to "the people of Freetown," and also to her editor Judith Jones "with many thanks for her deep understanding."

Edna proved to be that dream of any editor, the born writer. As with her cooking, she would instinctively assemble just the right group of a few words to sum up a perfect, evocative description of a simple recipe (far harder to describe than a more complex dish). Her recipes are still treasured today. A 2017 *Top Chef* television episode themed around *The Taste of Country Cooking* provoked a spike in sales to #3 on Amazon's bestselling cookbook list. The book is still in print (the thirteenth printing) and for any cook interested in authentic Southern cooking it remains a primary reference source.

The romantic appeal of Edna's childhood in the rural South has only increased since her day. "As children we looked forward eagerly to the ripening of wild strawberries, searching along fence rows and in fields along streams for the berries. It was unbelievable that anything so delicious could ripen so early in spring. They were fleeting—in a week they would appear and then be gone." The seasons of the year were marked by festive menus: A Late Spring Lunch after Wild Mushroom Picking, Midsummer Sunday Breakfast, a Race Day Picnic in the fall, and in winter A Dinner Celebrating the Last of the Barnyard Fowl. "On hot summer days between wheat harvesting and Revival," Edna remarks, "we would often enjoy an afternoon of feasting on homemade ice cream or a bowl of crushed peaches. It seemed that there was always something delicious to reward us at the end of any hectic work."

Edna Lewis was always active in the kitchen. After *Country Cooking* was published, she returned to restaurants and in 1988 published *In Pursuit of Flavor*, a further collection of Southern recipes of which she remarked: "I feel fortunate to have been raised at the time when the vegetables from the garden, the fruit from the orchard, and the meat from the smokehouse were all good and pure, unadulterated by chemical and long-life packaging. As a result, I believe I know how food should taste." With friends, Edna founded the Society for the Revival and Preservation of Southern Food. One member was Scott Peacock, a well-known chef of the Watershed Restaurant in Atlanta, Georgia, whom she had

DIVERSITY AND WOMEN
COOKBOOK AUTHORS

Edna Lewis was by no means the first black woman to publish a cookbook. In 1866, *A Domestic Cook Book: Containing a Careful Selection of Useful Receipts for the Kitchen* appeared in print, written by Malinda Russell, a former slave. The 150 recipes in its thirty-nine pages were brief, more pamphlet than book, but Malinda was a pioneer. She was in the vanguard of a troop of cookbook authors, both men and women, mostly white, who at the close of the Civil War were inspired to document the generous cooking of the antebellum South. The first full-scale cookbook written by a black woman was *What Mrs. Fisher Knows About Old Southern Cooking*, published in San Francisco in 1881 by Abby Fisher, a freed slave who sought a new life in California. She was illiterate but managed to convey into print "a book of knowledge—based on an experience of upwards of thirty-five years—in the art of cooking," containing more than 160 recipes. By the end of the twentieth century fewer than three hundred books on Southern cooking had been published that were credited to black writers of either gender. Their recipes are dominated by the most common Southern ingredients: pork, corn in all its guises, particularly grits, rice, peanuts, okra, mustard greens, and kale, often with a punch of chile pepper. In Louisiana, a particular style called Creole developed, based on a great mélange of Caribbean and Native American cooking with West African, Spanish, and French traditions. *The Welcome Table* by Jessica B. Harris, a professor and food historian, published in 1995, sums up the panorama with great authority.

On the West Coast, immigrant cooks stuck closer to the food of their cultural origins, whether it be Chinese, Italian, or Mexican. Very few ethnic cuisine cookbooks were published before the 1960s. Joyce Chen, one of the first acclaimed Asian-American chefs and cookbook writers, didn't publish her first book, the *Joyce Chen Cook Book*, until 1962.

By the close of the twentieth century, more cookbooks were appearing by women, many of whom ran market stalls or cookie shops, or who catered desserts, or baked fresh breads and cakes, driven to write about their professional expertise. As access to education and career paths opened up for all women, would-be cooks and cookbook authors blossomed. Today, we are familiar with seeing women from a multitude of cultural backgrounds cooking on television, publishing books, and running their own restaurants, and we celebrate the diversity of women cooks and cookbook writers.

met behind the stove when cooking at a charity event in 1990. Alice Waters describes seeing them on a similar occasion making pies one by one by hand. Edna and Scott taught cooking classes in New York and, as Edna grew older, Scott gradually became her caretaker. Together they wrote a last book, *The Gift of Southern Cooking*, published in 2003. She and Scott Peacock shared a house in Decatur, Georgia, and it was there that she died on February 13, 2006.

Edna Lewis was far more than just a fine writer and gifted cook, she became a public figure, celebrated as the first black woman cookbook writer to achieve fame throughout America and beyond. Much of her success was due to her intuitive understanding of ingredients and how to treat them in the pan and on the plate, a knowledge that was acquired before the industrialization of food. She has inspired succeeding generations of cooks, notably Alice Waters, founder of Chez Panisse restaurant in Berkeley, which has come to be known as the epicenter of California cuisine. Alice sourced local ingredients and producers, acknowledging Edna Lewis's influence from *Country Cooking* as showing the way to "the glories of an American tradition worthy of comparison to the most evolved cuisines on earth, a tradition of simplicity and purity and sheer deliciousness that is only possible when food tastes like what it is, from a particular place, at a particular point in time."

Quail in Casserole

The Taste of Country Cooking, 1976

Quail are small birds and we usually added other game near the end of cooking, sometimes a small chicken.

SERVES 4 TO 5

Stuffing
5 slices stale bread with the crusts removed
⅓ cup milk
Livers from quail and squab, finely chopped
¼ cup melted butter
¼ teaspoon sage
Salt and pepper

Casserole
6 quail
1 squab chicken
1 cup plus 3 tablespoons butter
3 slices bacon
Salt and pepper
¼ teaspoon thyme
½ pound mushrooms, sliced
½ pound seedless white grapes

Prepare the stuffing by soaking the slices of bread; put them in a dish and pour milk over, letting them stand a minute. Take the soaked slices two at a time, and squeeze tightly by hand. When all the milk is squeezed out, loosen the bread by pulling it apart with your fingertips. Mash the liver with a fork and mix well with the bread. Pour the melted butter over the bread mixture, sprinkle in sage, salt, and black pepper.

Prepare quail by wiping inside and outside with a damp cloth. (Washing game will take away some of the flavor peculiar to game.) Stuff the birds with the dressing and sew the opening up with a needle and thread (the stitches will be removed before serving). Rub them over with soft butter.

Wash the squab chicken under cold water and wipe dry. Have at hand a heavy iron or enamel casserole heating with 3 tablespoons of the butter. Heat up a second heavy skillet and add ½ cup of butter. When it is foaming, put in the squab chicken. Sear well on both sides and then place the squab in the center of the casserole, skin side down, spreading the bacon around it.

Quickly sear the quail in the same pan, then set the quail on top of the squab chicken. Sprinkle the birds lightly with thyme, salt, and fresh-ground pepper. Place on each bird a thin pat of butter. Set the pan into a preheated 350° oven for 45 minutes. Near the end of cooking, sauté the sliced mushrooms in about 3 tablespoons of butter for 4 to 5 minutes over a high flame, stirring. When the birds are done, take a heated platter and place the squab chicken in the center skin side up, arrange the quail around, and sprinkle the dish with the sautéed mushrooms. Squeeze ¼ cup of juice from the grapes and pour it into the pan the quail was cooked in. Loosen all particles on bottom and sides, blend well, and season to taste. Then pour this hot sauce around the quail. Serve hot.

QUAIL CASSEROLE WITH MUSHROOMS AND GRAPES

Quail have long been associated with grapes, because these little birds run around vineyards sheltering under the leaves. Quail meat is tender and slightly gamey. It's also sparse on the bone, so Edna adds a baby pigeon (also known as squab) to accompany her half-dozen quail. The contrast of the gamey squab and the more delicate quail is appealing, while the grapes provide both a garnish and juice to deglaze the pan for gravy. This is a sumptuous dish!

SERVES 6

For the stuffing
5 slices dry white bread, crusts removed
⅓ cup/75 ml milk
3 tablespoons butter, melted
Livers from quail and squab
2 or 3 chicken livers (about 2 ounces/60 g total)
Salt and pepper
2 or 3 leaves sage, chopped

For the casserole
6 quail, deboned (about ¼ pound/110 g each)
1 baby pigeon (squab), deboned (about ¾ pound/330 g)
Salt and pepper
3 tablespoons/45 g butter
3 slices bacon, halved
1 sprig thyme, leaves chopped
½ pound/225 g seedless white grapes
½ pound/225 g button mushrooms, sliced
Wooden toothpicks; large flameproof casserole; large skillet

1. Heat the oven to 350°F/175°C and set a rack low down.

2. Make the stuffing: Spread the slices of bread on a sheet pan, pour over the milk and leave to soak 2 to 3 minutes. Squeeze the bread and pull it into crumbs with your fingers, discarding the milk. In the skillet, heat 1 tablespoon of the melted butter, then add the livers (quail, squab, and chicken), season with salt and pepper, and sauté them, stirring, until lightly browned, 3 to 5 minutes. Let the livers cool, then chop them, discarding the membranes. Stir the livers, along with the sage and the remaining 2 tablespoons melted butter, into the bread crumbs. Taste and adjust the seasoning.

3. Wipe the inside of the quail and squab and pat them very dry with paper towels. (Do not wash the birds, as they will not brown well.) Fill the birds with the stuffing, packing it loosely, and fasten closed with toothpicks. Sprinkle the birds with salt and pepper.

4. In the casserole, heat 2 tablespoons of the butter over medium heat. Add the quail and brown on all sides, 8 to 10 minutes, until they are partially cooked. Take them out and set aside. Add the squab and brown over medium heat, then cover the pan and cook until partially cooked, about 15 minutes.

5. Lay the bacon pieces around the squab in the casserole, place the quail on top, and sprinkle with thyme. Cover, transfer to the oven, and bake until all the birds are thoroughly cooked, 10 to 15 minutes. A metal skewer inserted through each bird and the stuffing should be hot to the touch when withdrawn and the leg joints should be pliable. The squab may take longer than the quail and if so, cook it 8 to 10 more minutes.

6. Meanwhile, press half the grapes in a coarse sieve set over a bowl to extract about ¼ cup/60 ml of juice; discard the skins. In the skillet heat 1 tablespoon of the melted butter, add the mushrooms, season with a little salt and pepper and sauté until wilted, 2 to 3 minutes.

7. When the quail and squab are cooked, carve the squab in 6 pieces. Discard the toothpicks from the squab and the quail. Arrange the birds on a large platter with the quail encircling the squab. Sprinkle the mushrooms on top, cover, and keep warm. Set the casserole over medium heat and continue frying the bacon until crisp, then set a piece on top of each bird. Pour off and discard excess fat from the casserole, add the remaining grapes, along with the grape juice, and heat, stirring to deglaze the pan juices, for 1 to 2 minutes. Spoon the grape juice gravy and whole grapes over the birds and serve as a grand platter!

Crispy Biscuits

The Taste of Country Cooking, 1976

There were many variations in the making of biscuits to suit the particular occasion; for instance, for ring mold of chicken (see page 28) and casserole of quail, thin, crisp biscuits were more appropriate than the light soft ones we served at breakfast and other meals.

MAKES ABOUT 16 BISCUITS

¼ teaspoon salt
2 cups sifted unbleached flour, more for kneading
½ teaspoon baking soda
2 teaspoons Royal Baking Powder
5 tablespoons butter
⅔ cup sour milk or buttermilk

Sift the flour, salt, soda, and baking powder into a mixing bowl. Cut the butter into small pieces and add to the flour mixture. Blend this mixture with your fingertips or a pastry blender until it becomes grainy and heavy as cornmeal. Sprinkle in the milk and mix with a stout wooden spoon. Shape the dough into a ball and place it upon a lightly floured surface. Knead for a minute or two, giving quick, rolling punches into the dough. Then roll out to a ¼ inch thickness, pierce the dough over with a dinner fork, and cut it out with a 2-inch cutter. Place the biscuits about an inch apart on a heavy cookie sheet or baking pan. Set into a preheated 475°F for 10 to 12 minutes until nicely browned. Remove from the oven, let rest a minute or two, and serve hot.

CRISPY BUTTERMILK BISCUITS

Don't expect these to be big buttermilk biscuits; even a modest appetite will demand at least three. They are the size of silver dollars, and very tempting. Pair them with a thin slice of Smithfield ham or top with whipped cream and honey as a dessert with tea.

MAKES ABOUT FORTY 2-INCH/5 CM BISCUITS
ENOUGH FOR 8 TO 10 PEOPLE

2 cups/250 g flour, more for rolling
2 teaspoons baking powder
½ teaspoon baking soda
½ teaspoon salt
⅓ cup/75 g butter, cut in small dice, more for the
   baking sheet
⅔ cup/150 ml sour milk or buttermilk
2-inch/5 cm round cookie cutter

1. Heat the oven to 475°F/250°C and set a rack in the center. Butter a baking sheet.

2. Sift the flour, baking powder, baking soda, and salt into a bowl. Add the butter and mix with your fingertips until it is the grainy consistency of cornmeal. Sprinkle with the milk and stir with a wooden spoon until the dough comes together in a ball.

3. Turn the dough onto a floured work surface and knead it with quick, rolling punches for about 1 minute. This is not like kneading bread. A light touch is very important; avoid handling the dough too much as this will melt the butter.

4. Flour the work surface again and roll the dough to ¼-inch/5 mm thickness. Stamp out 2-inch/5 cm rounds with the cookie cutter and set them about 1 inch/2.5 cm apart on the baking sheet. Press the dough trimmings together and roll to make 2 or 3 more biscuits.

Bake until nicely browned, 10 to 12 minutes. Let cool a minute or two, then transfer the biscuits to a basket lined with a napkin. Wrap loosely and serve the biscuits while still hot. The biscuits will keep well until the following day.

Purple Plum Tart

The Taste of Country Cooking, 1976

Filling
1½ pounds purple plums
⅔ cup sugar

Pastry
1 lightly filled cup plus 2 tablespoons unsifted unbleached
    flour
¼ cup sugar
½ cup (1 stick) butter
¼ teaspoon salt
Grated rind of ½ medium-sized lemon
9-inch tart pan or shallow spring-bottom cake pan

Wash and drain plums, cut in halves, and discard pits. Place halves in a single layer skin side down in a flat casserole or ovenproof Corning Ware dish. Sprinkle over with ⅔ cup sugar. Set into a preheated 425° oven for about 15 minutes. This is to extract most of the juice. Remove from oven and set aside.

Place one cup of the flour, sugar, butter, salt, and lemon rind in a mixing bowl. Blend all together with fingertips and when well blended, knead the dough continuously for 15 minutes. This is the key to obtaining good results from this butter-rich dough. Sift in 1 tablespoon of flour during kneading and a second tablespoon near the end of kneading. This is a very soft dough.

Spoon it into an ungreased tart pan or spring-bottom cake pan. Lightly press as you push the dough evenly over surface of pan and around sides, making a rim of ½ to ¾ inch high and about ¼ inch thick.

Place the cooked plums skin side down on the pastry, reserving the juice. Arrange them to look attractive and set into moderate oven preheated to 350° for 20 to 30 minutes. The crust should be light brown in color. Remove from the oven, let cool. Set the juice that was extracted from the plums on the burner and reduce to a syrupy consistency, watching not to let it burn.

Spoon this over the plums. This should give a beautiful glaze. If you like, the tart can be garnished with a ring of whipped cream but it [sic] just as delicious without.

Note: Purple plums are usually plentiful when in season but do not hold very long. They deteriorate rapidly by drying out and losing their tart flavor. Therefore, get your supply early in the season. I chose plum tart over other fall fruits because I feel plums are the most fitting fruit for this butter-rich pastry. It is an easy fruit to find in city markets, but at home we used to make this tart also with regular pie dough. This particular pastry has been worked out after many trials, adjusting the quantities, the amount of kneading, and the oven temperature. Butter-rich doughs tend to dry out with the slightest overcooking; it is imperative that a strict watch be kept during the baking.

GLAZED PLUM TART

So much of this tart depends on the plums: They should be almost bursting at the seams with juice. Their season is short, but when the moment strikes, a rare treat awaits with this simple tart. The dough is like a sugar cookie, with only butter holding it together. Edna suggests a ring of whipped cream inside the rim of the tart as an optional decoration.

SERVES 6 TO 8

1½ pounds/675 g purple plums
⅔ cup/140 g sugar

For the pastry dough
1 cup/125 g flour, more for rolling
¼ cup/60 g sugar
1 stick/110 g butter, cut in dice, more for the pan
½ teaspoon salt
Grated zest of ½ lemon
9-inch/23 cm tart pan with removable bottom
   or shallow springform cake pan

1. Heat the oven to 425°F/220°C and set a rack in the center.

2. Wash and drain the plums, halve and pit them. Set the plums, cut side down and in a single layer, in a shallow baking dish. Sprinkle them with the sugar and bake until the juice runs freely, 12 to 15 minutes. Set the plums aside to cool, with their juice. Leave the oven on and reduce the temperature to 350°F/175°C.

3. Make the pastry dough: In a bowl, combine the flour, sugar, butter, salt, and lemon zest. With your fingertips, rub the ingredients together to form crumbs, then press them together into a ball of dough. Knead the dough in the bowl for 15 minutes, working in 1 to 2 tablespoons more flour if needed—it should be rich and sticky. (Alternatively, the dough can be mixed and kneaded with the dough hook of a stand mixer, allowing 3 to 5 minutes.)

4. Tip the dough into the ungreased tart pan and press it over the bottom and sides of the pan with your fist, making a rim that is ¾ inch/2 cm high and about ⅜ inch/8 mm thick. Arrange the cooked plums, cut side up and in concentric circles, on the dough, reserving the syrupy juice. Bake until the crust is lightly browned, 30 to 35 minutes.

5. Remove the tart from the oven and let it cool. Transfer the plum juice to a small saucepan and stir over medium heat, simmering until syrupy, 3 to 5 minutes—take care, as it burns easily. Spoon the syrup over the plums before serving.

Caramel Pie

The Taste of Country Cooking, 1976

Brown-sugar caramel pie is another local dessert, known and loved for at least a hundred and fifty years. The ladies of Freetown prided themselves on making the most perfect desserts. One neighbor was very proud of her talent; whenever we visited her she would bring out a pie or a tart, and as she served it, she would always say, "Taste it! It'll melt in your mouth!" and it would. This is a very haunting dessert, so rich and sweet one could easily overindulge. It's great after a heavy meal, to be served in tiny tarts or in very slender wedges.

MAKES 2 8-INCH PIES

Pastry dough, see page 217
Filling
3 cups soft dark-brown sugar (not brownulated)
⅛ teaspoon salt
2 tablespoons sifted flour
2 eggs, separated and beaten
2 tablespoons butter, slightly melted over hot water
4 tablespoons dark Karo syrup
2 teaspoons vanilla extract
1 cup milk, at room temperature
8-inch pie plates or tart pans

Line pie plates or tart pans with pastry and refrigerate.

In a large mixing bowl mix sugar, salt, and flour. Stir well with a clean wooden spoon and stir well again after each addition. Add the beaten yolks, butter, syrup, vanilla, and milk. When well mixed, beat the egg whites to soft peaks and fold in. Pour the batter into chilled, pastry lined pans. Set into a preheated

350° oven. Bake until set, about 35 to 40 minutes. Remove from the oven. Serve warm. When cut, the filling should be about the consistency of blackberry jelly, not too firm.

Pastry
2 cups sifted flour
½ teaspoon salt
½ cup cold lard
¼ cup cold water

Treat the same way as other two-crust pie pastries, page 41.

Put the sifted flour and the salt into a 2-quart bowl, add the chilled lard, and mix well with a pastry blender or with fingertips. This blend will not be as dry as a butter-mixed pastry. When well blended add all of the water and mix until the water is all absorbed. This will make the dough a bit sticky. Sprinkle over lightly with 2 teaspoons of flour and roll into a ball. Leave to rest for about 15 minutes.

BROWN SUGAR CARAMEL PIE

The silky filling for this pie is a dark caramel color and would pair wonderfully with a dollop of unsweetened whipped cream. Serve the pie in slivers, as it is very rich, and top it with a few fresh pecans.

MAKES TWO 10-INCH/25 CM PIES

For the pastry dough
2½ cups/300 g flour, more for sprinkling and rolling
1 teaspoon salt
⅔ cup/150 g lard, chilled and cut in dice, more for the pan
¼ cup/60 ml water, or more if needed

For the filling
3¾ cups/600 g dark brown sugar
3 tablespoons flour
½ teaspoon salt
4 eggs, separated
3 tablespoons butter, melted
⅓ cup/75 ml dark corn syrup
2½ teaspoons vanilla extract
1⅓ cups/325 ml milk
Two 10-inch/25 cm shallow pie pans or deep plates

1. Make the pastry dough: Sift the flour and salt into a bowl. Add the lard and rub it into the flour as lightly as possible with your fingertips. This will be a stickier dough than when butter is used. Sprinkle over the water and continue mixing until the dough comes together in a ball. If the crumbs seem dry, add more water. Sprinkle the dough lightly with additional flour, cover with a kitchen towel, and leave to rest about 15 minutes.

2. Divide the dough in half and shape each half into a ball. Sprinkle a work surface with flour and roll one ball of dough to a 10-inch/25 cm round. Line one of the pie pans with the dough, prick it all over and crimp the edge with a fork. Repeat with the other ball of dough and the other pie pan, then chill both pie shells in the refrigerator.

3. Heat the oven to 350°F/175°C and set a rack in the center.

4. Make the filling: In a bowl, stir together the brown sugar, flour, and salt. In a separate bowl, mix together the egg yolks, melted butter, corn syrup, vanilla, and milk. Stir the egg mixture into the sugar mixture. Stiffly whisk the egg whites, then fold them into the sugar mixture.

5. Pour the filling into the pie shells and bake until the pastry is lightly browned and the filling is set, 35 to 45 minutes. Serve the pies warm; the filling will still be quite soft.

Country-Fried Apples

The Taste of Country Cooking, 1976

SERVES 5 TO 6

6 apples
3 tablespoons fresh bacon fat
⅓ cup sugar

Prepare apples by peeling, quartering, coring and quartering again. Heat the bacon fat in a hot skillet and when sizzling add the apples. Cover and cook briskly until the apples become soft and there is juice in the pan. Timing depends on the type of apple you use, but you can tell the apples are soft when they begin to break up. Remove cover and sprinkle the sugar over the apples. Stir and cook with the cover off until the liquid has dried up and apples begin to brown. Cook medium-brisk until the apples are quite brown. Stir frequently. The apples should be a mixture of light and very dark amber.

FRIED APPLES

This recipe for caramelized apples fried in bacon fat relies on the apple holding its shape in the pan rather than dissolving into applesauce. Varieties like Fuji, Gala, or Pink Lady are good options here. Fried apples are delicious with rich meats, such as pork and duck, or for dessert, topped with a scoop of vanilla ice cream.

SERVES 4 TO 6

6 small apples (about 2 pounds/900 kg)
3 tablespoons bacon fat
⅓ cup/75 g sugar

1. Peel, quarter, and core the apples, then halve each quarter into crescents. Heat the bacon fat in a large skillet and when sizzling, add the apples, spreading them evenly in the skillet. Cover and cook briskly until they start to soften, 3 to 6 minutes, depending on the apple variety. Turn the apples, cover, and cook them on the other side, 1 to 2 minutes longer.

2. Sprinkle the apples with the sugar, stir, and cook over quite high heat until they start to brown and caramelize, 1 to 2 minutes. Turn again and continue cooking a minute or two longer, stirring often, until they are as brown as Edna Lewis describes. If the apples start to break up, stop cooking. Transfer them to a platter, spoon over the juices from the pan, and serve warm.

MARCELLA HAZAN

1924–2013

Marcella Hazan was born in Cesenatico,
down the coast from Venice on the Adriatic Sea.

RECEIPES

Chapter 11

MARCELLA HAZAN

The Classic Italian Cookbook

*The model for ethnic cookbooks, creating a new standard
for authentic Italian cooking in America.*

Marcella Hazan and Edna Lewis published their first cookbooks within
a year of each other in New York, and they shared an editor, but there
any connection ends. Edna Lewis was the daughter of the rural American South, Marcella was international, born in 1924 as Marcella Polini
in Cesenatico, a small Italian seaside town 120 miles south of Venice. Her father was a worldly tailor who spoke several languages, and
her mother, Maria Leonelli, came from an expatriate Italian family of
tobacco manufacturers from Beirut. Marcella herself was raised in Alexandria, Egypt, and must have been an adventurous child. At the age of
seven she was running on the beach, fell awkwardly, and broke her right
arm. Several surgeries later, her arm remained permanently bent and her
hand twisted into a fist, though she did learn to hold a knife, and taught
herself to write with her left hand. Marcella was tough, a survivor.

Marcella and her family returned to Cesenatico, where she spent her
teenage years. She went on to study in Venice, Padua, and Ferrara, and
by 1954 had achieved a double doctorate in biology. Nowhere along
the way did anyone mention Marcella's cooking abilities. Her life was a
string of train rides from classes to workshops in various cities, and on
one of the evening journeys she met Victor Hazan, a New Yorker who

had been born in Cesena, just eight miles from Cesenatico. Victor was working as a furrier with his father but he was more interested in literature and words, and he spoke with brilliance.

Marcella was bewildered to hear Victor talk about food, a subject she appreciated but took for granted. "I never thought about it," she says in her memoir, *Amarcord: Marcella Remembers*, published in 2008 (*amarcord* meaning "I remember" in her native Romagnolo dialect). "I accepted the pleasure that mealtimes at home always brought as a naturally recurring part of daily life." Victor changed all that. He moved into one of the rooms Marcella's parents rented out during the summer, living on a tiny allowance that his parents sent from New York. In late February 1955, Marcella and Victor were married and honeymooned on the shores of Lake Garda, their main remembrance of the hotel table being a steaming cauldron of leek and potato soup that Marcella found "miraculously reassuring."

Six months later the Hazans sailed for New York on the SS *Cristoforo Colombo*. Victor went back to the family business and Marcella found herself living in a small apartment in Forest Hills, Queens, without occupation, speaking no English—she retained a marked Italian accent all her life—and expected to cook for her husband, a connoisseur of fine food. Even the ingredients in the smattering of Italian-run stores in Manhattan's Little Italy appeared alien, with little relation to those at home. America seemed, remarked food writer Kim Severson in an article in the *New York Times* just after Marcella's death in 2013, "a country whose knowledge of her native cuisine was not much more than spaghetti covered with what tasted like overly spiced ketchup."

Undaunted, Marcella set about immersing herself in New York City. She would buy the voluminous Sunday *New York Times*, and try to absorb as much of it as she could. But she still found city life hard going. "The coffee tasted as though I had been served the water used to clean out the pot," she complained. She found sweet sauces with meat very strange, marveling at the tradition of serving cranberry sauce with the Thanksgiving turkey among other cultural novelties. Victor's copy of the classic Italian cookbook by Ada Boni, *Il talismano della felicità*, dating from 1929 became her bible. Whenever he could, Victor would come home for lunch, the main meal of the day in Italy, a custom that continued all their lives. Menus ran the traditional course of antipasti (often inexpensive but fresh vegetables), pasta (homemade on the circular wooden table in her apartment) or risotto, occasionally polenta, and then the main course. Tomato sauce was a standby and her first cookbook listed five variations, each with its own purpose: tomato sauce for macaroni; one each for gnocchi, penne, and ziti; plus an all-purpose simple version of tomato, butter, onion, and a pinch of salt and sugar, a sauce that is now synonymous with her name. The only food they did not share was chicken, which Victor detested. As her English improved, Marcella found a job in a research laboratory, and a couple of years later she gave birth to a son, Giuliano. (In 1986 Marcella dedicated *Marcella's Italian Kitchen* to Giuliano, calling him "her star pupil.")

Marcella didn't initially profit from her cooking, that came much later. In 1969 she enrolled in a Chinese cooking course with Grace Chu and must have impressed her fellow students because at the end of the six weeks they asked her to teach them some Italian cooking. On the face of it, she was not the ideal instructor: She was by nature cantankerous. But she knew, intuitively, how to teach. Marcella's career was launched by Craig Claiborne, the legendary food editor at the *New York Times*, who heard about her classes. He interviewed her in 1970, inviting himself to lunch, so Marcella cooked a meal to impress her illustrious guest. The menu included Artichokes alla Romana, their stems waving in the air, followed by tortellini stuffed with ricotta and Swiss chard, and a cold rolled veal roast with a salad of shaved fennel. There was no dessert, just sliced oranges sprinkled with a little bit of sugar. The resulting story occupied most of the food section front page. "I have never since then had to be concerned about how to occupy my time," wrote Marcella in her memoir. It must have been in the early '70s when I was writing for *The Washington Star* that I interviewed Marcella in her home. She was not much impressed by my French-trained approach to cooking. And my British accent cannot have helped either.

This was a propitious moment for cooking. Julia Child had just begun her triumphant career on television and the weakness of the national economy encouraged eating at home. After people learned to cook French food with Julia, Italy was an obvious next choice. Marcella jumped right in. With her damaged right hand, she always felt self-conscious on television, but the classes she gave at home, centered around her wooden dining table, became renowned, and bookings would sell out months in advance. Written recipes were a necessity and with Victor's help, Marcella developed an immensely readable style: "Never, never break spaghetti in two!" she cries, and on risotto, "Don't drown the rice. Remember, risotto is not boiled rice." She draws the cook into her kitchen, chopping, frying, tasting, all leading to the table.

Marcella's books are vivid proof of the difference in approach between the cooks of France and Italy. Both focus on local ingredients and both have a range of regional specialties—the rice of the Po Valley for instance, the polenta of northern Italy, and the cream and Calvados of Normandy. But the French have gone on to create an intellectual structure to their cooking, with the stocks and sauces, the elaborate pastries, the braises and estoufades, and overall a national ethos that is absent in Italy. The cooking has remained triumphantly local, whether Piedmontese, alla Romana, or alla Siciliana. "The first useful thing to know about Italian cooking is that, as such, it does not exist." So opens Marcella's first *The Classic Italian Cook Book: The Art of Italian Cooking and the Italian Art of Eating*, published by Alfred A. Knopf in 1973. She captures the essentially regional character of Beans and Sauerkraut Soup of Trieste, of slivers of calves' liver and onions called Fegato alla Veneziana, the Cappelletti (stuffed dumplings) served at Christmas in Romagna, and the Breaded Veal Chops of Milan. All can be found easily in its region, but are relative rarities elsewhere.

Marcella explains: "The cooking of Italy is really the cooking of its regions, regions that until 1861 were separate, independent, and usually states hostile to one another . . . they developed their own cultural traditions and, of course, their own special and distinct approaches to food." She defines the recipes by subject: antipasti (appetizers), i primi (first courses, a huge section that includes pasta, rice, and polenta), followed by main courses of fish, poultry, and meats, particularly veal. Vegetables and salads are emphasized: "I cannot imagine Italy without its vegetable stalls, filling ancient squares and animating dusty side streets with mounds of fabulous forms in purple, green, red, gold, and orange," writes Marcella. "In a land heavy with man's monuments, these are the soil's own masterworks." She herself is by inclination a cook of pasta and savory dishes, not a baker—in *The Classic Italian Cook Book*, desserts and fruits are sparse, just 21 out of a total of more than 250 recipes. The proportion reflects the Italian family habit of buying cakes, tarts, and gelati at the pastry shop; *nonna* (grandma) may make a treasured lemon tart, but that's about it.

When *The Classic Italian Cook Book* appeared, reviews were ecstatic: "A fascinating work . . . an indispensable volume for anyone who cares about Italian cooking," declared Craig Claiborne in the *New York Times*. "One of the finest Italian cookbooks ever to appear in English," said James Beard, and it went on to seven editions. The recipes are simple, clearly written, and easy to follow. One reason that Marcella was so successful was that she thought, and cooked, as if she were still in Italy. Another reason was Victor—the channel for her ideas and the means of expressing them in English. It was he who noted down recipes to her dictation, translating them and adding elegant, lively headnotes. He acted as her always courteous and well-appointed business agent. "Without his confidence I would not have started this work, without his support I would soon have abandoned it," she declares in her dedication to *The Classic Italian Cook Book*. In public they were often together, and my own memory has Victor always standing a step behind Marcella and smiling to offset her habitually stern expression.

Marcella Hazan and Julia Child were close contemporaries, though Marcella was younger and continued teaching until shortly before her death in the autumn of 2013. Julia was the master of cooking on television, Marcella was famous for her books and the practical cooking classes she gave both in New York and Venice, where she had an apartment overlooking the lagoon. The two women came from opposite sides of the kitchen in their approach to cooking. Julia believed in education and study, she read books and took lessons with master chefs. Marcella started at home and continued with that vision, cooking first by instinct and later from experience. In a conversation shortly before her death in August 2004, Julia Child told Mark Bittman, then a food writer at the *New York Times* and a proponent of minimalist cooking: "I don't get the whole thing with Italian cooking. They put some herbs on things, they put them in the oven and they take them out again." "That's exactly it," Bittman replied.

As they grew more prosperous, Victor and Marcella returned to Italy, running their cooking schools in Bologna and Venice with Marcella in the kitchen and Victor acting as guide on field trips. They continued to write half a dozen cookbooks, including *More Classic Italian Cooking* (1978), *Marcella's Italian Kitchen* (1986), and *The Essentials of Classic Italian Cooking* (1992), all published by Knopf. True to form, Marcella had several disagreements with Judith Jones, the editor she shared with both Edna Lewis and Julia Child. On some level, however, both editor and writer must have recognized each other's talents. When Marcella died in 2013, she left behind a handwritten manuscript called *Ingredienti*, her guide to selecting fresh produce and other key elements of Italian cuisine. Victor translated and transcribed the pages, and this loving tribute was published in 2016.

Today, nearly fifty years after *The Classic Italian Cook Book* appeared, it remains the definitive source on the cooking of Italy for an American audience. "Even people who have never heard of Marcella Hazan cook and shop differently because of her," declares Kim Severson.

Pomodoro al Forno
Oven-Browned Tomatoes

The Classic Italian Cook Book, 1973

In this recipe, all the wateriness of fresh tomatoes is drawn off through long, slow cooking. What remains is a savory, concentrated essence of tomato.

Don't let the quantity of oil alarm you. Nearly all of it gets left behind in the pan.

FOR 6 PERSONS

9 ripe, medium tomatoes or 6 large ones, such as the beefsteak variety
3 tablespoons finely chopped parsley
2 teaspoons finely chopped garlic
Salt to taste
Freshly ground pepper, about 6 to 8 twists of the mill
6 tablespoons olive oil, or enough to come ¼ inch up the side of the baking dish

1. Wash the tomatoes in cold water and slice them in half, across the width. If the variety of tomatoes you are using has a large amount of seeds, remove at least a part of them.

2. Preheat the oven to 325°.

3. Choose a flameproof baking dish large enough to accommodate all the tomato halves in a single layer. (You can crowd them in tightly, because later they will shrink considerably.) Arrange the tomatoes cut side up and sprinkle them with the parsley, garlic, salt, and pepper. Pour the olive oil over them until it comes ¼ inch up the side of the dish. Cook on top of the stove over medium-high heat until the tomatoes are tender, about 15 minutes, depending on the tomatoes.

4. When the tomato pulp is soft, baste with a little bit of oil, spooning it up from the bottom of the dish, and transfer the dish to the next-to-the-highest rack in the oven. From time to time baste the tomatoes with the oil in which they are cooking. Cook for about 1 hour, until the tomatoes have shrunk to a little more than half their original size. (The skins and the sides of the pan will be partly blackened, but don't worry—the tomatoes are not burned.) Transfer to a serving platter, using a slotted spatula, leaving all the cooking fat behind in the pan. Serve hot or at room temperature.

NOTE: These tomatoes can be prepared several days ahead of time. Since they must be reheated, they should be refrigerated with all or part of their cooking fat. When refrigerating, cover tightly with plastic wrap. To reheat, return to a 325° oven for 10 to 15 minutes, or until warm.

MENU SUGGESTIONS: This dish is a tasty accompaniment to roasts and to Mixed Broiled Meats (page 322). You would never use it, of course, next to any dish already sauced or flavored with tomato. Nor does it get along well with cream or milk sauces. Its perfect marriage is with Fried Eggplant (page 372), when both are at their peak, in midsummer, and the two make a sensational combination as a side dish with Breaded Veal Cutlets (page 270).

ROASTED TOMATOES

Olive oil and garlic are natural partners to the great big ripe tomatoes that are essential to this recipe. Be sure it is tomato season! They can be served hot as a side dish or cool as an appetizer.

SERVES 6

6 large tomatoes (½ to ¾ pound/225 to 330 g each)
6 tablespoons/90 ml olive oil
2 to 3 cloves garlic, chopped
3 to 4 tablespoons chopped parsley
2 teaspoons salt
Freshly ground black pepper
9 x 13-inch/23 x 32 cm baking dish

1. Heat the oven to 325°F/160°C and set a rack in the center.

2. Wipe the tomatoes with damp paper towels and scoop out the cores. Halve the tomatoes through the equator to reveal the seeds. Gently squeeze the halves to loosen and discard some of the seeds. Pack the tomatoes, cut side up, in the baking dish. Spoon the olive oil over the tomatoes and sprinkle them with garlic, parsley, salt, and pepper to taste.

3. Bake the tomatoes until they are browned, tender, and shrunken with split skins, 50 to 60 minutes. From time to time during cooking, baste the tomatoes with the oil and juices in the baking dish. Serve hot or at room temperature.

Polenta con la Luganega
Polenta with Sausages

The Classic Italian Cook Book, 1973

FOR 1 TO 6 PERSONS

2 tablespoons chopped yellow onion

3 tablespoons olive oil

3 tablespoons chopped carrot

3 tablespoons chopped celery

¼ pound sliced pancetta, cut into strips ½ inch wide

1 pound luganega sausage or other sweet sausage, cut into 3-inch
   lengths

1 cup canned Italian tomatoes, cut up, with their juice

Polenta (previous page)

1. Put the onion in a saucepan with the oil and sauté over
   medium heat until pale gold.

2. Add the carrot, celery, and pancetta. Sauté for 3–4 minutes,
   stirring frequently.

3. Add the sausages and cook for 10 minutes, always at medium
   heat, turning them from time to time.

4. Add the tomatoes and their juice and cook at a gentle simmer
   for 25 minutes, stirring from time to time. Cover the pan
   and transfer to a 200° oven to stay warm while you prepare
   the polenta.

5. When the polenta is done, pour it onto a large platter. Make
   a depression in the center and pour in the sausages and all
   their sauce. Serve immediately.

MENU SUGGESTIONS: This is a second course, but
polenta takes the place of pasta or rice, so you can omit

the first course. It is quite appropriate to precede this with a plate of mixed Italian cold cuts, such as prosciutto, good salami, and mortadella. Another excellent antipasto would be Peppers and Anchovies (page 37).

BASIC METHOD
FOR MAKING POLENTA

1 tablespoon salt
2 cups coarse-grained cornmeal

1. Bring 6½ cups water to a boil in a large, heavy kettle.

2. Add the salt, turn the heat down to medium low so that the water is just simmering, and add the cornmeal in a very thin stream, stirring with a stout, long wooden spoon. The stream of cornmeal must be so thin that you can see the individual grains. A good way to do it is to let a fistful of cornmeal run through nearly closed fingers. Never stop stirring, and keep the water at a slow, steady simmer.

3. Continue stirring for 20 minutes after all the cornmeal has been added. The polenta is done when it tears away from the sides of the pot as you stir.

4. When done, pour the polenta onto a large wooden block or a platter. Allow it to cool first if you are going to slice it in preparation for subsequent cooking. Otherwise, serve it piping hot.

NOTE: It may happen that some of the polenta sticks to the bottom of the pot. Cover the bottom with water and let it soak for 25 minutes. The polenta will then wash away easily.

POLENTA
WITH ITALIAN SAUSAGES

Whether you prefer yellow or white cornmeal, this makes for a colorful main dish that is bright with tomatoes and carrot. For me, the cornmeal must be coarsely ground with a slightly crunchy texture.

SERVES 4 TO 6

¼ cup/60 ml olive oil
1 small onion, chopped
1 carrot, chopped
1 stalk celery, chopped
¼ pound/110 g pancetta, cut in wide strips
1 pound/450 g sweet Italian sausages, cut into
    3-inch/7.5 cm lengths
1 cup/225 g chopped canned plum tomatoes
Salt and pepper
2 cups/340 g yellow or white polenta
1½ quarts/1.5 liters water

1. In a medium saucepan, heat the oil over medium heat. Add the onion and fry until starting to brown. Add the carrot, celery, and pancetta and continue cooking, stirring often, until the vegetables are soft, 2 to 3 minutes. Add the sausages and cook, turning them often, until they are lightly browned, 2 to 3 minutes. Add the tomatoes and continue simmering, stirring often, until no pink juices run from the sausages when they are pierced with a two-pronged fork, 12 to 15 minutes. Taste and adjust the seasoning. Keep the sausage mixture warm.

2. Put the polenta in a bowl. In a medium saucepan, bring the water to a boil with 1 tablespoon salt. Keep it at a simmer, stirring constantly with a wooden spoon. With the other hand, take a fistful of cornmeal and let it drizzle in a thin stream into the boiling water. Stir in all the cornmeal in this way. Continue simmering, stirring

constantly, until the cornmeal is cooked but retains a slight bite, 5 to 8 minutes depending on the coarseness of the meal.

3. Pour the cornmeal onto a deep platter, make a depression in the center, and add the sausage mixture, arranging the sausages around the edges. Serve at once.

Risotto with Beef, Rosemary, Sage, and Barolo Wine, Alba Style

Essentials of Classic Italian Cooking, 1992

FOR 6 SERVINGS

5 cups Basic Homemade Meat Broth, prepared as directed
on page 15, OR 1 cup canned beef broth diluted with 4
cups water

3 tablespoons butter

3 tablespoons pancetta chopped very fine

1½ teaspoons garlic chopped very fine

Chopped rosemary leaves, 1½ teaspoons if fresh, ¾
teaspoon if dried

Chopped sage leaves, 2 teaspoons if fresh, 1 teaspoon if
dried

¼ pound ground beef chuck

Salt

Black pepper, ground fresh from the mill

1⅓ cups Barolo wine (see note below)

2 cups Arborio or other imported Italian risotto rice

⅓ cup freshly grated parmigiano-reggiano cheese, plus
additional cheese at the table

NOTE: Barolo, perhaps Italy's greatest red wine, and certainly its most profound in flavor, can satisfactorily be replaced in this preparation by its closest relative, Barbaresco. For other substitutions, look for wines derived from the same distinctive nebbiolo grape, such as Gattinara, Spanna, Carema, or Sfursat. You could try still other red wines, and although you might well make an excellent risotto with them, it would not be this risotto.

1. Bring the broth to a very slow, steady simmer on a burner near where you'll be cooking the risotto.

2. Put 1 tablespoon of butter, the pancetta, and the garlic in a broad, sturdy pot, turn on the heat to a medium high, and stir from time to time as you cook. When the garlic becomes colored a very pale gold, add the rosemary and sage, cook and stir for a few seconds, then add the ground meat. Crumble the meat with a fork, and turn it over several times to brown and coat it well, adding salt and a generous grinding of pepper.

3. When the meat has been well browned, add 1 cup of the red wine. Cook to a simmer, letting the wine bubble away until it becomes reduced to a film on the bottom of the pan.

4. Turn up the heat, add the rice. Stir quickly and thoroughly until the grains are coated well.

5. Add ½ cup of simmering broth, and cook the rice following the directions in Steps 3 and 4 of the basic white risotto recipe [on page 245]. When the rice is just about done, but still rather firm, after approximately 25 minutes, add the remaining wine, and finish cooking, stirring constantly, until all the wine has evaporated.

6. Off heat, add the 2 tablespoons of butter and the grated Parmesan, and stir thoroughly, turning the risotto over and over until the cheese has been well distributed and has melted. Taste and correct for salt. Transfer to a platter and serve promptly, with additional grated cheese on the side.

RISOTTO FROM ALBA

The town of Alba, home of white truffles, lies in the hills of Piedmont in central Italy, with rice growing in the nearby valley of the Po River. In early autumn, finely sliced fresh truffles will be showered over risottos such as this one. Some cooks prefer their finished risotto to be moist and flowing *al onda*, on the wave, others like the rice to hold a soft shape; it should never be sticky. At the end of the cooking, a slight crunch may be left in the rice or it may be completely tender, again a matter of taste. Risotto in the style of Alba can be a first course, or the accompaniment to a main course of veal or beef. A robust Italian wine is important in this recipe, both for flavor and color, and it is well worth looking for one of the bottles that Marcella suggests.

SERVES 6

2 cups/500 ml mild beef stock
3 cups/750 ml water, more if needed
3 tablespoons/45 g butter
3 oz/90 g pancetta, very finely chopped
1 clove garlic, chopped
1 sprig rosemary, the leaves chopped
2 to 3 sage leaves, chopped
4 oz/110 g ground beef
Salt and pepper
1½ cups/375 ml Barolo or other robust red wine
2 cups/400 g Arborio or risotto rice
½ cup/75 g grated Parmesan cheese
Sauté pan or other shallow pan

1. In a saucepan, bring the stock and water to a simmer and keep just at a simmer at the back of the stove.

2. In the sauté pan, melt 1 tablespoon of the butter over medium heat. Stir in the pancetta and garlic and cook until fragrant, stirring with a wooden spoon, 3 to 5 minutes. Stir in the rosemary and sage, then the ground beef, breaking up the meat with a fork. Season with salt and pepper, and stir until the meat has lost its red color, 3 to 5 minutes. Add 1 cup of the wine and simmer, stirring, until reduced to a glaze but still moist.

3. Increase the heat to medium high and add the rice, stirring with a

wooden spoon until the grains are coated. Add a ladleful of stock and cook, stirring constantly, until the liquid has evaporated. Continue adding stock and stirring constantly so that the rice gradually becomes fragrant and translucent, 20 to 25 minutes. When the risotto is done, most but not necessarily all the stock and water will be used.

4. When the rice is cooked to be firm or slightly crunchy, runny or holding a shape, depending on your taste, take the pan from the heat. Stir in the remaining ½ cup wine, 2 tablespoons butter, and the Parmesan. Taste, adjust the seasoning, and serve.

Granita di Caffè con Panna
Coffee Ice with Whipped Cream

The Classic Italian Cook Book, 1973

A granita is a dessert made of very fine-grained frozen crystals of coffee or fruit syrup. By far the most popular granita in Italy is granita di caffè, coffee ice. It is usually taken at a cafe after lunch, and, as you sit outdoors on a steamy afternoon watching life flow by, you let the granita melt between tongue and palate, spoonful by spoonful, until the inside of your mouth feels like an ice cavern dense with coffee flavor.

It should go without saying that you use only Italian espresso coffee to make granita di caffè.

FOR 6 TO 8 PERSONS

2 cups espresso coffee (see How to Make Italian Coffee, page 455)
2 tablespoons sugar, or more to taste
Freshly whipped cream, made with 1 cup heavy cream and 2 teaspoons sugar (optional)

1. Put all the coffee in a pitcher and dissolve the sugar in it while it is still hot. Taste and correct for sweetness. Do not make it very sweet because sugar weakens its flavor.

2. Remove the ice-cube grids from two freezer trays and pour the coffee into the trays. When the coffee is cold, put the trays in the freezer and set a timer at 15 minutes.

3. When the timer rings, remove the trays from the freezer and stir the contents to break up the ice crystals. (Ice forms first at the sides of the tray. It is important that you break this up thoroughly each time before it becomes solid.) Return to the freezer, and set the timer again for 15 minutes. When the timer rings repeat the operation and reset the timer for 10

minutes. The next time set the timer for 8 minutes, and continue to stir the coffee every 8 minutes for the next 3 hours. If you are not ready to serve the granita immediately, continue stirring every 8 minutes until just before serving. Serve in a glass, goblet, or crystal bowl, topped with whipped cream, if desired.

NOTE: By exactly the same procedure, you can make orange ice (granita di arancia), using 2 cups freshly squeezed orange juice and 1 tablespoon granulated sugar, and lemon ice (granita di limone), using ½ cup freshly squeezed lemon juice, 1½ cups water, and ¼ cup granulated sugar.

ESPRESSO GRANITA

Just one ingredient is key to this simple, sophisticated dessert: fresh espresso. So heat up your home machine and be prepared to make two cups of a concentrated brew. A rimmed metal baking sheet is best for freezing the granita, which is topped with a cloud of whipped cream. This recipe requires intermittent attention, so make it when you're busy elsewhere in the kitchen. The achievement is well worth it!

SERVES 6 TO 8

2 tablespoons sugar, or more to taste
2 cups/500 ml freshly brewed espresso coffee

For serving
1 cup/250 ml heavy cream
2 teaspoons sugar (optional)
Glass bowls or stemmed glasses; 7 x 8-inch/
  18 x 22 cm rimmed metal tray

1. Stir the sugar into the hot espresso, adding more if you wish. (Too much sugar will mask the brisk coffee flavor of the dessert.) Pour the coffee into a rimmed metal baking tray and set it in the freezer. Stir it often, every 15 minutes, using two forks held upright in your hands. This breaks up the ice crystals and after about 2½ hours, they will be the consistency of crunchy snow.

2. Meanwhile, for serving: Whip the cream until it holds a soft peak, then whisk in the sugar if using. Keep the cream chilled. Chill the serving glasses.

3. If possible, serve the granita within 15 minutes, or else keep stirring often. Just before serving, top each glass with whipped cream.

ALICE WATERS

1944–

Alice Waters pulls a radish in her garden.

Chapter 12

ALICE WATERS

Chez Panisse Menu Cookbook

*A cookbook that celebrates the national movement
toward local ingredients and seasonal eating.*

Alice Waters took America back to its roots. Marcella Hazan had reintroduced cooks to the joys of fresh ingredients instead of the dreary commercial packages that had been the norm from the 1950s, but she was confined to the rubric of Italian cooking. Alice went much further, insisting not only that fruits and vegetables should be fresh, but also that they should be locally grown. "She has had so much to say about how the rest of us ought to eat that it's been easy to assume that she always had a master plan to transform the American diet . . . with mesclun and goat cheese," says Pete Wells, in a *New York Times* book review of Alice Waters's memoir, *Coming to My Senses: The Making of a Counterculture Cook,* published in 2017. But the master plan had been long in the making.

Alice Louise Waters was born in 1944 in a clapboard house in Chatham, New Jersey, the second daughter of four. Her parents were left-wing intellectuals, and dinner at the automat was her birthday treat. The family occasionally went into Manhattan, but most of the time Alice was playing baseball with the boys, and left feminine pursuits to her sisters. At school her grades were good but she was "distractible," she says. "I talked to my friends too much, and the teachers would put me in the coatroom to punish me." She loved jelly doughnuts and homemade coconut ice cream. Her favorite lunch was a grilled cheese sandwich with pickles on the side, "one of the great comfort foods," she remarks in her memoir.

When Alice was a teenager, her father was transferred to Chicago then to California, so she had a final high school year in Los Angeles followed by college in Santa Barbara. Her first real job was waitressing with her friend Eleanor in Sherman Oaks, California, where the turkey was roasted in-house, and she still remembers the taste of the bacon and avocado sandwich on toasted cheese bread. UC Berkeley followed, and with it activism. Alice moved to the Bay Area in 1963, the year that President Kennedy was assassinated. "Berkeley in January 1964 was a complete shock," admits Alice. "I looked into this room [a bookstore] and saw people lying on the couches, draped all over, smoking God knows what, doing God knows what drugs. I felt a little shaken. . . . Have I made the right decision?"

The turning point for Alice came in 1965 when she and a friend, Sara Flanders, spent their junior year abroad taking the Cours de Civilisation Française at the Sorbonne in Paris. America seemed far away, and Alice became enthralled with the French approach to food. She and Sara happened to find lodgings in the Quartier Latin on the rue Mouffetard, where the daily outdoor market was, and is, a famed institution dating back hundreds of years. The produce is gathered, often early that morning, in the fertile Île-de-France gardens that ring southern Paris.

Alice ate cheese at almost every meal and became obsessed with it: fresh cheese, aged cheese, blooming, runny cheeses made with cow, sheep, and goat's milk; she explored how to age cheeses and how to serve them. She herself always enjoyed cheese with salad, a habit that was quite new in France at the time. Later she came to know Jan d'Alos, a cheese *affineur* whose stock on display might include a couple dozen varieties of cheese, but whose cellar contained, says Alice, "hundreds upon hundreds of wheels of cheeses, and he knows the exact moment to bring each one out."

When Alice returned to Berkeley, counterculture continued to rage, which suited her. She joined the Free Speech Movement and worked for the Congress of Racial Equality. She cooked with friends, buckwheat crêpes being a specialty, and worked in a little restaurant called Quest where the owner did all the cooking himself and played Chopin on the piano. It was here, inspired by her time in France, that the seeds were sown for Chez Panisse. The name came from the widower Panisse, a gourmand character in a Marcel Pagnol film. In France, Alice had learned to eat, a talent that never left her, and when she returned to Berkeley she often watched Julia Child. After all, Julia loved France, and so did Alice: "I've always said that Julia Child's show allowed Chez Panisse to flourish. And that's the truth—if Julia hadn't prepared people for French cooking, our little French restaurant never would have worked."

Julia's show may have helped provide the customers for the opening of Chez Panisse in 1971, but Alice's high standards kept the restaurant in the red for eight long years; it was loans from friends that kept it going. Alice was determined to create meals that used only locally grown, seasonal ingredients, provided by farmers whom she would get to know personally. The early years of Chez Panisse coincided with a fundamental revolution in the way Americans eat. No longer were two, possibly three, structured meals taken with family or friends around a table. More and more, Americans were eating several smaller snacks, often standing, walking in the street, or driving in the car. Offshoots of this moment include the birth of Starbucks in Seattle and other European-style cafes. In addition to starting a new business, Alice was fighting against a cultural wave, and it took time. She opened with an inexperienced staff and, like many small restaurants in France, a menu that changed daily. This had the advantage of showcasing the freshest ingredients at their peak, but in the kitchen each day was different and it was hard to establish a routine.

Just three years earlier than Alice, I, too, had discovered the magic of Paris. I went to l'École du Cordon Bleu, intending to stay three months, but lingering for two years. I ended at the Château de Versailles, teaching the Mexican cooks of the curator, Gerald Van der Kemp, and his American wife, Florence. Down in this international basement we cooked for the likes of President Charles de Gaulle and the Duke and

Duchess of Windsor. Alice Waters and I share a love for French cooking, but we come to it from different sides. I admire French gastronomic structure, their enthusiasm for regional and historical cooking. I'm amused by their periodic diversions into nouvelle cuisine, *cuisine minceur* (diet cooking), *cuisine moléculaire*, and the eccentric French approach to barbecue. Alice is a practical cook; she takes these trends on board and runs her own way with them. She knows the rules and adapts them accordingly.

The philosophy behind Chez Panisse was different, too, even revolutionary: Women were treated the same as men. It was "cultural and aesthetic, built on domestic arts that were generally the domain of women," comments Pete Wells, "not the professional skills of the men who ran fancy restaurant kitchens." In 1968, Alice spent a year in London studying at the Montessori School where "learning by doing" is the active, practical principle. It suited her ideally and she followed its principles when she opened Chez Panisse. There was no printed and bound menu; like visiting a private home, you showed up and ate what was set before you. Alice has a gift for creating extemporary menus from ingredients on hand, one of the reasons that Chez Panisse was so successful. Her *Chez Panisse Menu Cookbook* (1982) is full of fresh combinations such as a summer menu of Tomato and Arugula Salad, Yellow Squash and Blossom Soup, Grilled Whole Filet of Beef with Deep-Fried Onion Rings, and Honey Ice Cream with Lavender. In those early days you would see Alice chopping and slicing at the counter that divided the tables from the kitchen, and you could stop and chat, though Alice had little spare time.

From the start, Alice's friend Lindsey Shere looked after the pastry side of Chez Panisse, for twenty-six long but happy years. Lindsey's recipes often centered on a single ingredient—chocolate, wine, dried fruits—and she was renowned for her Almond Tart and her Apple Galette with its wafer-thin slivers of fruit. For many years, Jeremiah Tower was the executive chef. A great number of gifted young cooks who later became famous were trained at Chez Panisse—Paul Bertolli, David Tanis, Jonathan Waxman, and Suzanne Goin among them—but relying on novice cooks is not a path that leads easily to profit. Never mind. "Profit was always secondary," declares Alice in the introduction to *Chez Panisse Menu Cookbook.*

Alice's husband, Stephen Singer, did not enter her life until the mid-1970s, and his unstructured style as a wine consultant suited Alice's erratic, intense way of life. They had a daughter named Fanny, and two years later, in 1985, were married in a ceremony in which Fanny was a flower girl; they later divorced. Alice's book *Fanny in France* (2016) evokes a summer in France with teenage Fanny, the cooking overseen by "My Mom's Special French Rules," such as shop at farmers' markets, plant a garden, and start each meal with a toast: Salut!

Alice remained close to her own parents. Her father had visited in the early days of Chez Panisse and was enthralled by the organization—or lack of it—of the restaurant. He was a human resources psychologist by profession, and his feedback intrigued Alice and her staff. He convinced Alice that Chez Panisse could have an overarching administration that he called "organic leadership."

The careers of Julia Child and Alice Waters were not so very far apart in time. *The French Chef* was launched in 1963, while Chez Panisse opened in 1971, but the two women were worlds apart both in age and philosophy. "After our little French restaurant had been open for a decade or so, I filmed an episode with Julia," recalls Alice. Julia, with her emphasis on traditional French techniques, must have been determined to pin down Alice's random approach to cooking. "We were a funny pair," confesses Alice, "Julia was over six feet tall and I am five foot two, so she towered over me. I was clearly not preparing food the way a chef was supposed to—and she knew it. I was pitting olives with my fingers, and she'd say, in that fluting voice of hers, 'Oh! Is that how you pit an olive, Alice? How fascinating!'"

Alice has long been a force in fund-raising for charity, insisting that "Feeding children is a moral issue." In 1996, twenty-five years after the opening of the restaurant, she launched the Chez Panisse Foundation and created the Edible Schoolyard Project, a one-acre garden at Berkeley's Martin Luther King Jr. Middle School, designing it as a blueprint for others across the nation. The ten principles of the "Philosophy of Alice Waters" are posted in the schoolyard, including: "Set the table with care and respect. Eat together. Food is precious." She urged Bill Clinton, who was then the president, to review the cheerless state of school lunches, and she found a true kindred spirit in Michelle Obama, who installed an organic garden at the White House and welcomed schoolchildren to plant and harvest vegetables and fruits as part of her anti-obesity campaign. With Michelle Obama's strong support, the Healthy, Hunger-Free Kids Act was passed in 2010 to improve school nutrition. "Probably the greatest lesson I have learned from the Edible Schoolyard Project is that, when children grow food and they cook it, they all want to eat it," comments Alice.

Alice has been given many, many awards, at least half a dozen for her cookbooks. In 1992 she won the James Beard Award for both Outstanding Chef and Outstanding Restaurant. In 1997 the James Beard Foundation named her Humanitarian of the Year, and in 2004 the award was for Lifetime Achievement. The French Légion d'Honneur came in 2009, with the IACP Lifetime Achievement Award in 2013. In 2014 she was honored by President Obama with the National Humanities Medal, an award given each year to a handful of contributors to the creative or performing arts.

Alice is an inveterate collector of books on cooking and gastronomy, crediting their contents for her inspiration in founding Chez Panisse. Certainly she would agree with Brillat-Savarin's adage, "We are what we eat." Many traits in Alice's cooking are revealed in her books, especially her enthusiastic approach to fruits and vegetables. In *Chez Panisse Vegetables* (1996), mushrooms, for example, earn three closely packed pages of information before ten recipes such as Chanterelle Pasta, Wild Mushrooms Baked in Parchment, and Potato, Morel, and Onion Fricassée. *Chez Panisse Fruit* (2002) starts predictably with apples, but goes on to include olallieberries, cape gooseberries, citron, dates, figs, pomelos, huckleberries, kumquats, loquats, mulberries, passion fruit, ending with rhubarb and strawberries (so often combined in the pan, but not here). Again and again she reiterates, "Good food depends almost entirely on good ingredients." And by "good" she means very, very fresh with a local provenance. Her style is didactic, crystal clear, and both books are designed and beautifully illustrated with paintings by Patricia Curtan.

In a short television interview with Gwen Ifill on PBS, Alice summed up her credo, "When you eat fast food, you not only eat food that is unhealthy for you, but you digest the values that come with that food. And they're really about fast, cheap, and easy. It's so important that we understand that things can be affordable, but they can never be cheap, because if they're cheap, somebody's missing out. The fast food culture tells us that, you know, cooking is not something important . . . I think it is the unrealistic values of a fast food culture that are really making us very unhappy, that we're all going a little crazy. We spend as much time searching on our cell phone as we do preparing a meal."

Alice Waters is an inspired, prolific writer of more than twenty books on cooking. These are not only cookbooks, though many are based on written recipes. She stands on the shoulders of earlier evangelists like Julia Child and Marcella Hazan in declaring that we can, and must, follow certain principles. For Alice, her meals are based on fresh, organic, locally grown ingredients that are treated with respect in the kitchen. Alice considers cooking as a means of communication and enjoying good company. She is acutely aware of the moral implications of her work. She is not without critics, as what she is advocating is also a luxury of privilege, a reward that she attempts to address in her Edible Schoolyard Project. For Alice, fine cooking is a statement of belief, a respect for nature, an enjoyment of friends and good company, a link to the earth. She is a restaurateur, a chef, a teacher, a fund-raiser, a philanthropist, and winner of America's highest national honor. Like the other cookbook authors profiled in this book, she is a remarkable woman.

BACK TO THE FARM

From the beginning of printed cookbooks some five hundred years ago, fresh ingredients were assumed to be local. Fruits and vegetables were grown in the back garden if there was one, or bought in the nearest market. A glance at the market stalls or on the dinner table would reveal location and time of the year; there was little question of carrying perishable ingredients more than a dozen miles. Flour was ground locally, too, each miller supplying a circle of customers at a maximum one day's journey from the mill itself, so bread would taste subtly different from place to place. In cities such as London, specialty markets developed: Billingsgate for fish near the river Thames, and meat at Smithfield, where herds were driven from the countryside for slaughter.

Starting in the mid-nineteenth century, railroads revolutionized transport so that markets for fresh meats, fish, and produce grew larger and less regionalized. Eventually refrigerated railroad cars made the fragile lettuce grown in California available three days later in the markets of downtown Manhattan.

For most restaurateurs and even domestic cooks, the concept of the seasons became less and less relevant. By the latter half of the twentieth century, almost every imaginable fruit or vegetable was available year-round, transported by airplane from different parts of the globe. The quality of such merchandise is debatable, however; robust fruits such as apples may be held for months at low oxygen levels, and some tomatoes have been developed with extra-thick skins, then picked weeks in advance so they ripen during transport.

A backlash to such practices was inevitable. Starting appropriately in southern California where so much produce is grown, outdoor farmers' markets began to reappear in the early 1990s. The movement has bloomed throughout the United States. The value of locally grown ingredients has become widely acknowledged and its participants have even coined a name, locavores. Sellers in farmers' markets are licensed, and strict rules govern the provenance of what is sold. There are now more than seven hundred farmers' markets in America, and in Europe the scene is even brighter. There weekly outdoor markets date back to medieval times and beyond, securing the livelihood of producers who make regular progress from place to place each week, as they have begun to do again in America. Cooks around the world are turning back to such small-scale farmers, recognizing they are the key to flavor and good food.

Fig and Grape Salad
with Pancetta Crostini

Chez Panisse Fruit, 2002

Of course, this tastes best made with an authentic, costly, artis-anally made balsamic vinegar (the kind labeled "aceto balsamico tradizionale di Modena" and bearing the seal of the produc-ers' consortium), but it can be approximated by using instead a reduction of good commercial balsamic vinegar.

3 tablespoons artisanally made balsamic vinegar, aged 12 years
    or more. Or ½ cup good-quality commercial balsamic
    vinegar plus 1 teaspoon brown sugar
6 thick slices country-style bread
Extra-virgin olive oil
12 thin slices pancetta (about ¼ pound)
9 ripe figs
1 cup grapes stemmed (wine grapes, if available)
6 small handfuls arugula
Salt and pepper

If substituting commercial balsamic vinegar, put it in a small saucepan with the brown sugar and reduce by a little more than half, until the vinegar is thick and syrupy.

Preheat the oven to 375°F.

Trim the crusts off the bread and cut the slices in half length-wise, making 12 long, thin crostini. Brush them lightly with olive oil and wrap with slices of pancetta—spirally, like candy canes. Place them on a baking sheet and bake them until the pancetta begins to crisp, about 10 minutes.

While the pancetta-wrapped crostini are baking, quarter the figs, cut the grapes in half, and thoroughly wash and dry the arugula. When the pancetta crostini are almost ready, gently toss the arugula and fruit with a pinch of salt, a few grinds of the peppermill, and about 3 tablespoons olive oil. Arrange the salad on plates and drizzle with the balsamic vinegar. Garnish with the crostini. Serves 6.

CHEZ PANISSE FIG AND GRAPE SALAD

Figs and grapes ripen at the same time, making them ideal partners for this very Californian appetizer.

SERVES 4 TO 6

½ cup/125 ml balsamic vinegar
1 teaspoon brown sugar
2 tablespoons olive oil, more for the baking sheet
  and brushing the bread
6 thick slices country bread
12 thin slices (about ½ pound/225 g) pancetta
9 black figs
1 cup/about 225 g seedless black or green grapes
4 cups arugula (about ½ pound/225 g)
Salt and pepper

1. In a small saucepan, mix the vinegar and brown sugar. Bring to a boil and simmer until reduced and the vinegar is thick and syrupy, 4 to 5 minutes. Set it aside to cool.

2. Heat the oven to 375°F/190°C and set a rack in the center. Brush a baking sheet with oil.

3. Cut off and discard the crusts from the bread, then brush the bread slices with olive oil and cut them crosswise into sticks. Wrap the pancetta slices spirally around the sticks like candy canes. Set these crostini on the baking sheet and bake until the pancetta and bread begin to crisp, 15 to 20 minutes.

4. Meanwhile, quarter the figs and halve the grapes. Combine the fruit and arugula in a bowl with about 2 tablespoons of olive oil. Sprinkle with salt and pepper and toss the salad; taste a leaf of arugula and adjust the seasoning.

5. Pile the salad on 4 to 6 serving plates and drizzle with the reduced vinegar. Top each plate with 2 or 3 crostini. Serve while still warm.

Mango Salad with Hot Pepper

Chez Panisse Fruit, 2002

SERVES 6.

2 large ripe mangos
½ red onion
1 fresh habanero chili, or ½ teaspoon ground cayenne pepper
¼ cup lime juice (2 or 3 limes)
Salt
¼ cup chopped cilantro (leaves and stems, about ½ bunch)
A few sprigs cilantro

Peel the mangos with a small sharp knife. Cut the flesh away from the mangos following the directions on page 165 [see below]. Cut the mangos lengthwise into ¼-inch slices. Thinly slice the onion. Cut the habanero chili in half and remove the stems and seeds. Chop the chili into a fine dice. Wear rubber gloves if you wish to protect your hands from the pepper.

Gently toss the mango, onion, and chili or cayenne pepper with the lime juice, a bit of salt, and the chopped cilantro. Taste for salt and acid and adjust as needed. Chill for half an hour. Garnish with cilantro sprigs before serving.

[From page 165]

Mangos have a single large, flat seed in the center of the fruit clinging tightly to the flesh. Which must be cut away from the seed with a knife. This can be done before or after peeling. Stand the fruit on its stem end, narrow side facing you. Allowing about three-quarters of an inch as the thickest part of the pit, cut off the "cheeks" of flesh on either side of the pit, which is about three-quarters of an inch thick. Cut as close to the pit as possible, but avoid the very fibrous flesh near its surface. You can then cut away the two thinner strips of flesh that remain on the pit. Peel and cut or puree the fruit as needed.

MANGO SALAD WITH CHILE PEPPER

Firm mangoes are needed for this colorful salad, but they must still be ripe enough to smell delicious. The onion must be wafer thin so it falls into fragile rings. Habanero chilies are notoriously hot, so unless you know them well, you may prefer to use dried cayenne pepper, also very hot but much easier to control.

SERVES 6

2 large mangoes
½ sweet red onion
1 fresh habanero chile or ½ teaspoon cayenne pepper
1 medium bunch cilantro
Juice of 2 or 3 limes (3 to 4 tablespoons)
¼ teaspoon salt, or to taste

1. Peel the mangoes with a vegetable peeler or small knife. Holding them upright, stem end down, cut off the "cheeks," allowing about ¾ inch/2 cm on each side of the pit. Cut each cheek vertically into ¼-inch/5 mm slices and put them in a bowl. Cut the remaining mango flesh from the pits, discard the pits, dice the flesh, and add to the slices. Thinly slice the onion. If using a fresh chile, halve it lengthwise, discard the core and seeds, and very finely chop the flesh. Strip the cilantro leaves from the stems, set aside half a dozen for garnish and chop the rest.

2. Sprinkle the sliced onion over the mangoes. Sprinkle in most of the chopped chile or cayenne, lime juice, and salt. Add the chopped cilantro, toss the salad, and taste, adding more chile, lime juice, or salt if needed. Refrigerate for 30 minutes before serving. Garnish each plate with a sprig of cilantro.

Cured Grilled Salmon Vinaigrette

Chez Panisse Menu Cookbook, 1982

SERVES 6

1 whole fillet of salmon, about 2 pounds
¼ cup coarse salt
6 3-inch tarragon sprigs

Lay a 2-pound fillet of salmon skin side down, and sprinkle with ¼ cup coarse salt. Place 6 sprigs of tarragon on top of the salt. Put the salmon skin side up in a lightly oiled dish and cover with a damp tea towel. Refrigerate for 1 day.

For the Vinaigrette
1 shallot
10 to 12 chives
12 to 14 sprigs chervil
¾ cup light olive oil
Juice of 1 lemon, or to taste
Salt and pepper
1 cucumber (Japanese, if available)

To make the vinaigrette, dice 1 shallot very finely and mince 10 to 12 chives. Remove the leaves from 12 to 14 sprigs of chervil. Mix the shallot and herbs with ⅔ cup of the olive oil and lemon juice to taste. Season with salt and pepper. Wash the cucumber and cut it into thin slices.

Take the salmon out of the refrigerator ½ hour before serving. Remove the salt and tarragon from the salmon and peel off the skin. Prepare a wood charcoal fire. Brush the salmon lightly with olive oil on both sides and put it on a hot grill for 2 to 3 minutes on each side, until it feels firm and springy when pressed with a finger. It should be quite rare in the center. Toss the cucumber slices with the vinaigrette and divide them on six serving plates. Cut the grilled salmon into thin slices and serve it with the cucumber salad.

CURED SALMON WITH
CUCUMBER SALAD

King salmon, rich and firm, is good for this recipe. Cooking time depends very much on the thickness of the fillet. The king of fish cookery, James Beard, specifies 10 minutes of cooking per 1 inch/2.5 cm of thickness, or a bit less if you like your salmon rare. Chervil can be hard to find, but parsley is a good alternative.

SERVES 6

1 large skin-on salmon fillet (about 2 pounds/900 g)
¼ cup/90 g coarse salt
6 sprigs tarragon

For the vinaigrette
1 medium bunch chervil
1 shallot, finely chopped
10 to 12 chives, finely chopped
Juice of 1 lemon, or more to taste
¾ cup/175 ml olive oil, more for grilling
Salt and pepper
1 Japanese cucumber, or regular cucumber

1. To cure the salmon, lay the fillet skin side down and sprinkle with the coarse salt. Put the tarragon sprigs on the salt and transfer the fillet to a lightly oiled shallow dish. Flip the fillet so the skin is facing up, cover with a damp kitchen towel and refrigerate for 1 day.

2. Half an hour before serving, light the grill or broiler.

3. Make the vinaigrette: Pull the leaves from the chervil, chop them, and put in a small bowl. Add the shallot, chives, lemon juice, and salt and pepper to taste. Whisk in the olive oil, taste, and adjust the seasoning. Peel and thinly slice the cucumber on the diagonal.

4. To cook the salmon, take the fillet from the refrigerator and wipe off the salt and tarragon. Brush both sides with olive oil and set the salmon, skin side down, on the grill (or skin side up under the broiler). Grill (or broil) until the salmon is lightly browned, 2 to 3 minutes, then flip and cook it 2 to 3 minutes longer with the skin facing the heat. When done, the fillet should feel firm and springy to the touch. Use a fork to peek inside the salmon, making sure it is rare or well done, to your taste.

5. Toss the cucumber slices with the vinaigrette and divide among six serving plates. With a narrow, sharp knife, and working from the head end toward the tail end, cut the salmon in thin slices. Arrange the salmon slices on the plates and serve.

Garlic Soufflé

Chez Panisse Menu Cookbook, 1982

SERVES 6

6 tablespoons unsalted butter

5 tablespoons all-purpose flour

1½ cups half and half cream

1 cup whipping cream

Salt

Bouquet garni: 1 small onion, peeled and quartered; 2 to 3
   cloves unpeeled garlic; ½ teaspoon dried thyme; 1 bay
   leaf; 4 sprigs parsley; 10 black peppercorns

2 large heads garlic

about ½ cup light olive oil

about ½ cup water

2 to 2½ tablespoons dried thyme

2 bay leaves

5 egg yolks

3 ounces freshly grated Gruyère

5 ounces freshly grated Parmesan

1 heaping tablespoon of the garlic purée

Salt, cayenne, and black pepper to taste

1 cup beaten egg whites

Make a roux of the butter and flour and cook it gently for 5 to
8 minutes. Mix the creams and scald them. Remove the roux
from the heat and cool slightly before whisking in the scalded
creams. Transfer the resulting béchamel to a double boiler and
salt it lightly. Tie the onion, 2 to 3 cloves garlic, ½ teaspoon dried
thyme, 1 bay leaf, 4 sprigs parsley, and 10 black peppercorns
in cheesecloth. Add the bouquet garni to the béchamel, cover,
and cook slowly for about 1 hour, stirring occasionally. Cool the

béchamel slightly and remove the bouquet garni before adding the rest of the soufflé ingredients.

For the garlic purée, break up 2 heads of garlic. Put the garlic in a shallow baking dish and barely cover with the olive oil and water. Stir in ½ teaspoon dried thyme and 2 bay leaves and season with salt and pepper. Cover the dish and bake at 250°F. for about 1½ hours, or until the garlic is completely tender. Baste the garlic often while it is baking. When the garlic is done, strain it from any remaining liquid and purée it through a food mill, or push it through a medium-fine sieve with a pestle.

Stir the 5 egg yolks into the béchamel. Mix 3 ounces Gruyère, 2 ounces of the Parmesan, and a generous tablespoon of the garlic purée. Season the mixture with salt, cayenne, and black pepper, and blend well. Butter some gratin dishes well (either one 12-inch oval platter with a slight lip or six 6-inch low gratin dishes) and coat them lightly with a little Parmesan cheese.

Beat the egg whites very stiff and fold three quarters of them into the cheese-garlic mixture. The mixture should be fairly loose, but not runny. (If it is runny, add more egg white.) Pour the soufflé gently into the prepared platter or individual gratin dishes. Sprinkle with the remaining Parmesan cheese, and then with the rest of the dried thyme over the Parmesan. Bake on the top shelf of a preheated 450°F. oven for approximately 10 minutes. The platter allows the soufflé to cook more quickly than a regular soufflé dish and provides more browned crust. The soufflé in the small gratin dishes will cook in about the same amount of time. The top and sides of the soufflé should be well-browned, and the inside warm and creamy.

GARLIC AND PARMESAN SOUFFLÉ

The age of the garlic, fresh and fragrant, or more mature and pungent, makes a big difference to its flavor; either is delicious in this recipe. You can make the puréed garlic and cheese base an hour or so ahead of time. (Note that the garlic takes more than an hour to roast before it gets puréed.) Shortly before you are ready to sit down, whisk the egg whites, mix them into the base, and bake the soufflé. Serve it at once—a soufflé does not wait for the diner!

SERVES 6

For the garlic purée
2 large heads garlic, divided into cloves and unpeeled
2 tablespoons dried thyme
2 bay leaves, crumbled
½ cup/125 ml olive oil
½ cup/125 ml water, or more if needed

For the cream sauce
1½ cups/375 ml light cream
1 cup/250 ml whipping cream
Bouquet garni: 3 or 4 parsley stems, 2 or 3 sprigs
    thyme, and 1 bay leaf, tied with string
6 tablespoons/90g butter
⅓ cup/45 g flour
Salt (optional)

For the soufflé mixture
Butter for the ramekins
5 egg yolks
3 ounces/90 g grated Gruyère cheese
5 ounces/140 g grated Parmesan cheese, more for the ramekins
Cayenne pepper
Black pepper
Salt (optional)
8 egg whites
1 tablespoon chopped fresh thyme leaves, for topping
6 (1-cup/250 ml) ramekins or a 1½-quart/1.5-liter soufflé dish

1. Make the garlic purée: Heat the oven to 250°F/120°C and set a rack in the center.

2. Spread the garlic cloves, dried thyme, and crumbled bay leaves in a baking dish and pour over the olive oil and water to barely cover them. Cover with foil and bake, stirring often to keep the garlic moist, until very tender, about 1½ hours. (If baking the soufflés right away, leave the oven on and increase the temperature to 425°F/220°C.) When done, strain and discard any remaining liquid and work the garlic through a medium sieve to remove the skins. There should be 2 to 3 tablespoons of purée; set it aside.

3. Meanwhile, make the cream sauce: In a saucepan, scald the light cream and whipping cream with the bouquet garni and set aside to infuse for 15 to 20 minutes. Discard the bouquet garni.

4. In a saucepan, melt the butter over medium heat. Whisk in the flour and cook gently, stirring often, 1 to 2 minutes. Whisk in the scalded cream and bring the sauce to a boil, whisking constantly until it thickens. Simmer, stirring often, for 1 to 2 minutes to cook the flour. Remove from the heat and let cool to tepid. Taste the sauce and adjust the seasoning.

5. Heat the oven to 425°F/220°C. Generously butter the ramekins or soufflé dish and sprinkle with grated Parmesan cheese.

6. Make the soufflé mixture: Whisk the egg yolks into the cooled cream sauce. Stir in the garlic purée, the Gruyère, and half the Parmesan. Season to taste with cayenne and black pepper—salt may not be needed as the cheeses are salty. Stiffly whip the egg whites and fold about one-quarter into the cheese mixture. Add the lightened cheese mixture to the remaining egg whites and fold together as lightly as possible. Fill the ramekins or soufflé dish level to the top and run a palette knife over the tops to level the soufflé mixture. Sprinkle with the remaining Parmesan and the fresh thyme. Set the ramekins or soufflé dish on a baking sheet and bake until puffed and brown, 12 to 15 minutes for the ramekins or 20 to 25 minutes for the soufflé dish. When done, the soufflés should still wobble slightly, showing

that they remain soft in the center and will form a sauce for the crisp browned outside.

7. Arrange the ramekins or soufflé dish on serving plates or a large platter lined with paper napkins to prevent the dishes from slipping when serving.

Epilogue

WHERE WE GO FROM HERE

In the nearly sixty years that I have been cooking professionally, women have burst out of the domestic kitchen. Opportunities for women have expanded in many directions, and with them their cookbooks. Now women are running restaurants, catering companies, commercial pastry shops, and other cooking businesses. Women are particularly gifted in photography and the styling of food on the plate. Women have long been the physicians in the family so that today's dietetics and vegetarian and vegan preparations are natural sidelines. And like their forebears in the domestic kitchen, today's women cooks are eager to share and to publish their skills and recipes. We enjoy passing on our knowledge to others. When I opened a school in Paris in 1975 to teach French cooking to foreigners, everyone thought I was crazy but École de Cuisine La Varenne (as it was called) survived thirty years and turned out thousands of students who I would like to think shared my own view of the importance of culinary structure. Most of our students were women and in those early days of liberation we were a welcoming place where they could find their feet in the kitchen in what was then a man's world.

The biggest change in the last fifty years has been the escalating careers of professional women chefs. Alice Waters was early in the field, but Edna Lewis had preceded her in the 1950s and she was by no means the first. In France, starting in the 1930s, a whole generation of women cooks was led by a group in Lyon known as *les mères* (the mothers), who shopped each morning at the market stalls along the banks of the Saône River and cooked in nearby bistros known as *bouchons*. But this mini-revolution did not extend to America until after Julia Child had revived French cooking at home.

It was with television, and later the Internet, that food became global. The French nouvelle cuisine movement of the 1970s relaxed the hierarchy that had so long been established by male chefs. The food was lighter, the ingredients quickly prepared, and arranged directly on the plate by the cook—in the style of a domestic kitchen. Such informality suited women cooks, and the cookbooks from that era take a simple approach with few, fresh ingredients, often with inventive seasonings. Ethnic dishes increased, authenticity became imperative, and the wide range of restaurants in most cities, from Mexican to Mediterranean, Indian to Thai, became a matter of course. As women do the cooking in many countries in the restaurants as well as at home, it was no surprise to see them behind many of these multicultural stoves.

Women have established not only a place in restaurant kitchens, but they have brought a more personal style at home. The same approach also marks their presence in their cookbooks, but here the market is sharply divided. In general, a cookbook may be written for the reader (who may or may not be a trained cook) who is already expert and yearns to hear the inside story from, say, a Deborah Madison or an Ina Garten. Alternatively, a cookbook author may be more of a teacher, appealing to the novice enthusiast who has been drawn in by an enjoyment of a good restaurant meal, or perhaps a television series, whether from the domestic goddess Nigella Lawson or the professionally trained Mashama Bailey.

Ironically, as women entered the professional kitchen, men began to invade the domestic cookbook sphere. Craig Claiborne and James Beard began the trend in the 1950s, and now in the food section of the bookshop Mark Bittman's books on simple cooking sit alongside those by Alice Waters, while journalists like Michael Pollan rub shoulders with the likes of Dorie Greenspan.

This said, the criteria for a successful cookbook by a woman has not changed since Hannah Woolley in 1661. The recipes must be clearly written, preferably with a strong personal voice, and with appeal to the style of eating of the day, whether family meals or fine dining. An eye for trends is useful, but nothing dates more quickly than pink peppercorns or sky blue frosting. Mandatory is thorough testing of the recipes in a domestic kitchen. From the beginning, good connections have been advantageous for the author, such as the aristocratic sponsors of the early days who have gradually morphed into support from a television channel or, less prestigious but more lucrative, a commercial food brand. If the author opens up about her personal story, on the Internet with her blog or website, or establishes herself on YouTube or Instagram so much the better. Above all, the author herself must know what she wants to say and how to say it, combining charm and a clarion call to action in the kitchen. Nothing tempts a reader into the kitchen like a golden gratin with its bubbling coat of melted cheese, or the invitation of a lofty layer cake just waiting to be sliced with a stout knife.

The recipe writer who can both inspire and guide the cook from start to triumphant finish is bound to succeed. The dozen gifted and successful women profiled in this book span four hundred years of activity in the kitchen, but the underlying principle of recording their knowledge for future cooks has not changed. Long may it continue to prosper.

BIBLIOGRAPHY

I have found the following works very helpful in learning about old cookbooks and compiling this book. *The Oxford English Dictionary* is a constant reference, plus the landmark 11th edition of the *Encyclopedia Britannica* (1910). Also very useful are the journals of *Petits Propos Culinaires* (Prospect Books).

Seventeenth Century

Culpeper, Nicholas. *Culpeper's Complete Herbal* [1653]. Reprint: London: Richard Evans, 1815. Modern edition: *Culpeper's Complete Herbal.* Chatham, England: Wordsworth, 1998.

Digby, Sir Kenelm. *The Closet Opened* [1669]. Reprint: London: H. C. for H. Brome, 1677. Modern edition: *The Closet of the Eminently Learned Sir Kenelme Digbie, Kt., Opened.* Edited by Peter Davidson and Jane Stevenson. Totnes, England: Prospect Books, 1997.

Evelyn, John. *Acetaria; A Discourse of Sallets* [London: For B. Tooke, 1699]. Modern edition: *The Rusticall and Economical Works of John Evelyn: Acetaria, A Discourse of Sallets.* Edited by Christopher Driver. Totnes, England: Prospect Books, 2005.

Grey, Elizabeth, Countess of Kent. *A True Gentlewomans Delight* [1653]. Reprint: bound with *A Choice Manual, or Rare and Select Secrets in Physick and Chirurgery.* London: Gartrude Dawson, 1665.

Lawson, William. *The Countrie Housewife's Garden* [London, 1617]. Reprint: London: Anne Griffin for John Harrison, 1637. Modern edition: Milford, CT: Salt Acres, 1940. Facsimile edition: *A New Orchard and Garden with The Country Housewife's Garden.* Totnes, England: Prospect Books, 2003.

Markham, Gervase. *The English House-wife* [1615]. By "G. M." Reprint: London: W. Wilson for George Sawridge, 1664. Modern edition: Gervase Markham, *The English House-wife.* Edited by Michael R. Best. Montreal: McGill-Queen's University Press, 1986.

BIBLIOGRAPHY

Eighteenth Century

Bradley, Mrs. Martha. *The British Housewife: or, the Cook, Housekeeper's and Gardiner's Companion* [London: For S. Crowder and H. Woodgate, 1755]. Modern edition: *The British Housewife*. Edited by Gilly Lehmann. Totnes, England: Prospect Books, 1996.

Carter, Susannah. *The Frugal Housewife* [1772]. Reprint: London: For E. Newbery, n.d.

Eales, Mary. *Receipts* [London: H. Meere, 1718]. Modern edition: *Mrs. Mary Eales's Receipts*. Totnes, England: Prospect Books, 1985.

Harrison, Sarah. *The House-Keeper's Pocket-Book, and Compleat Family Cook. Containing above Three Hundred Curious and Uncommon Recipes*. London: T. Worral, 1733.

La cuisinière bourgeoise [1746]. Reprint: Paris: Guillyn, 1748.

Moxon, Elizabeth. *English Housewifery* [1749]. Reprint: Leeds: For George Copperthwaite, 1758.

Smith, Mrs. E. *The Compleat Housewife* [1727]. Reprint: London: For J. and H. Pemberton, 1742.

The Compleat Confectioner. London: Mrs. Ashburn, 1760.

Nineteenth Century

Beecher, Catherine. *Miss Beecher's Domestic Receipt Book* [1846]. Reprint: New York: Harper & Brothers, 1851. Modern edition: Mineola, NY: Dover, 2001.

Beeton, Isabella. *The Book of Household Management* [London: S. O. Beeton, 1861]. Modern edition: *Mrs Beeton's Book of Household Management: Abridged Edition*. Edited by Nicola Humble. Oxford: Oxford University Press, 2000.

Randolph, Mrs. Mary. *The Virginia Housewife: or, Methodical Cook* [1824]. Reprint: Washington, DC: Way & Gideon, 1825. Modern edition: *The Virginia Housewife*. Richmond, VA: Avenel Books, n.d.

Vicaire, Georges. *Bibliographie Gastronomique*. London: Holland Press, 1890.

Twentieth Century

Aresty, Esther. *The Best Behavior: The Course of Good Manners—From Antiquity to the Present—As Seen through Courtesy and Etiquette Books*. New York: Simon and Schuster, 1970.

Beck, Leonard N. *Two "Loaf-Givers" or A Tour through the Gastronomic Librar-*

ies of Katherine Golden Bitting and Elizabeth Robins Pennell. Washington, DC: Library of Congress, 1984.

Bitting, Katherine Golden. *Gastronomic Bibliography.* San Francisco. 1939.

Brown, Peter, and Ivan Day. *Pleasures of the Table: Ritual and Display in the European Dining Room, 1600–1900.* York: York Civic Trust, 1997.

Cooper, Anne, *A Woman's Place Is in the Kitchen: The Evolution of Women Chefs.* New York: Van Nostrand Reinhold, 1998.

Davidson, Alan, *The Oxford Companion to Food.* Oxford: Oxford University Press, 1999.

Davidson, Caroline. *A Woman's Work Is Never Done: A History of Housework in the British Isles 1650–1950.* London: Chatto & Windus, 1982.

Hartley, Dorothy. *Food in England.* London: Macdonald, 1954.

Hess, John L., and Karen Hess. *The Taste of America.* Columbia: University of South Carolina Press, 1989.

Hess, Karen. *The Carolina Rice Kitchen: The African Connection.* Columbia: University of South Carolina Press, 1992.

Karcher, Carolyn, L.,ed. *A Lydia Maria Child Reader,* Durham and London: Duke University Press, 1997.

Lowenstein, Eleanor. *American Cookery Books 1742–1860.* New York: American Antiquarian Society, 1972.

Mendelson, Anne. *Stand Facing the Stove: The Story of the Woman Who Gave America the Joy of Cooking.* New York: Scribner, 1996.

Mennell, Stephen. *All Manners of Food: Eating and Taste in England and France from the Middle Ages to the Present.* Oxford: Basil Blackwell, 1985.

Paston-Williams, Sara. *The Art of Dining: A History of Cooking and Eating.* London: National Trust, 1999.

Revel, Jean François. Culture and Cuisine: A Journey through the History of Food. New York: Doubleday, 1982.

Shapiro, Laura. *Perfection Salad: Women and Cooking at the Turn of the Century.* USA and Toronto, Canada. Collins Publishers. 1986.

Symons, Michael. *A History of Cooks and Cooking.* Urbana: University of Illinois Press, 1998.

Tannahill, Reay. *Food in History.* New York: Stein and Day, 1973.

Visser, Margaret. *Much Depends on Dinner: The Extraordinary History and Mythology, Allure and Obsessions, Perils and Taboos of an Ordinary Meal.* New York: Grove, 1986.

Wheaton, Barbara Ketcham. *Savoring the Past.* Philadelphia: University of Pennsylvania Press, 1983.

Wilson, C. Anne. *Food & Drink in Britain: From the Stone Age to Recent Times.* London: Constable, 1973.

BIBLIOGRAPHY

Twenty-First Century

Albala, Ken. *The Banquet*. Urbana: University of Illinois Press, 2007.

Girouard, Mark. Life in the English Country House. New Haven, CT: Yale University Press, 1978.

———. *Life in the French Country House*. London: Cassell, 2001.

Lehmann, Gilly. *The British Housewife: Cookery Books, Cooking and Society in Eighteenth-Century Britain*. Totnes, England: Prospect Books, 2003.

Reardon, Joan. *As Always, Julia. The Letters of Julia Child and Avis DeVoto. Food, Friendship and the Making of a Masterpiece*. Boston and New York: Mariner Books, 2010.

RECIPE PERMISSIONS

Irma Rombauer

From THE JOY OF COOKING by Irma S. Rombauer and Marion Rombauer Becker. Copyright © 1931, 1936, 1941, 1942, 1943, 1946, 1951, 1952, 1953, 1962, 1963, 1964, 1975 by Simon & Schuster, Inc. Copyright 1997 by Simon & Schuster, Inc., The Joy of Cooking Trust and The MRB Revocable Trust. Reprinted with the permission of Scribner, a division of Simon & Schuster, Inc. All rights reserved.

Julia Child

"Ratatouille," "Coq Au Vin," "Thon à la Provençale," and "La Tarte des Demoiselles Tatin" from *Mastering the Art of French Cooking, Volume 1,* by Julia Child, Louisette Bertholle, and Simone Beck, copyright © 1961 by Alfred A. Knopf, a division of Penguin Random House LLC. Used by permission of Alfred A. Knopf, an imprint of the Knopf Doubleday Publishing Group, a division of Penguin Random House LLC. All rights reserved.

"Potage Velouté aux Champignons" from *Mastering the Art of French Cooking, Volume 2* by Julia Child and Simone Beck, copyright © 1970 by Alfred A. Knopf, a division of Penguin Random House LLC. Used by permission of Alfred A. Knopf, an imprint of the Knopf Doubleday Publishing Group, a division of Penguin Random House LLC. All rights reserved.

Edna Lewis

"Caramel Pie," "Purple Plum Tart," "Quail in Casserole," "Crispy Biscuits," and "Country-Fried Apples" from *The Taste of Country Cooking* by Edna Lewis, copyright © 1976 by Edna Lewis. Used by permission of Alfred A. Knopf, an imprint of the Knopf Doubleday Publishing Group, a division of Penguin Random House LLC. All rights reserved.

RECIPE PERMISSIONS

Marcella Hazan

Alice Waters

INDEX

INDEX